State of Illinois

**The Illinois School Law, 1889-1895**

State of Illinois

**The Illinois School Law, 1889-1895**

ISBN/EAN: 9783744667012

Printed in Europe, USA, Canada, Australia, Japan

Cover: Foto ©Suzi / pixelio.de

More available books at **www.hansebooks.com**

# THE ILLINOIS SCHOOL LAW.

## 1889-1895.

AN ACT TO ESTABLISH AND MAINTAIN A

# SYSTEM OF FREE SCHOOLS,

APPROVED MAY 21, 1889.

_____

INCLUDING ADDITIONAL ACTS RELATIVE TO SCHOOLS AND
SCHOOL OFFICERS, WITH AN APPENDIX CONTAINING ACTS
ESTABLISHING STATE NORMAL SCHOOLS, AND PRO-
VIDING FOR COUNTY NORMAL SCHOOLS.

SPRINGFIELD, ILL.
Ed. F. Hartmann, State Printer.
1895

# TABLE OF CONTENTS.

PAGE.

EXTRACTS FROM THE CONSTITUTION ............................................................ 1

ACT OF 1889.
Article I, State Superintendent of Public Instruction ......................................... 3
Article II, County Superintendents........................................................... 7
Article III, Township Trustees of Schools.................................................... 14
Article IV, Township Treasurer............................................................... 32
Article V, Board of Directors................................................................ 40
Article VI, Board of Education.............................................................. 48
Article VII, Teachers....................................................................... 55
Article VIII, Revenue—Taxation.............................................................. 61
Article IX, Bonds. .......................................................................... 64
Article X, County Clerk ..................................................................... 67
Article XI, County Board.................................................................... 69
Article XII, School Funds.................................................................... 71
Article XIII, School Lands................................................................... 74
Article XIV, Fines and Forfeitures........................................................... 80
Article XV, Liability of School Officers ..................................................... 82
Article XVI, Miscellaneous................................................................... 86

ADDITIONAL ACTS PERTAINING TO THE PUBLIC SCHOOLS AND TO SCHOOL
    OFFICERS.

Members of the Board of Education Appointed.................................................. 90
Study of Physiology and Hygiene............................................................. 91
Compensation of Judges and Clerks of Election in certain cases.............................. 92
Election of Boards of Education in certain cases............................................ 92
No child under 13 years of age to be hired without certificate from School Board ........... 94
Women may vote at School Elections.......................................................... 95
Directors allowed to assume indebtedness created for their districts........................ 95
Compulsory Attendance....................................................................... 96
Inspectors elected under certain special acts............................................... 97
Kindergarten................................................................................ 98
U. S. Flags ...........................................................................102-103
Pension and Retirement Fund in Certain Cities .............................................. 99

APPENDIX.

Act Establishing Central Normal University, Normal.......................................... 99
Act Establishing Southern Normal University, Carbondale.................................... 102
Act Establishing Eastern Normal School, Charleston........................................ 112
Act Establishing Northern Normal School, DeKalb........................................... 116
State Scholarships in Illinois University .............................................121-122
Act for the Establishment of County Normal Schools........................................ 119
Index .................................................................................123-131

# EXTRACTS FROM THE CONSTITUTION OF ILLINOIS.

## ARTICLE V.

SECTION 1. The executive department shall consist of a Governor, Lieutenant Governor, Secretary of State, Auditor of Public Accounts, Treasurer, Superintendent of Public Instruction and Attorney General, who shall each, with the exception of the Treasurer, hold his office for the term of four years, from the second Monday of January next after his election and until his successor is elected and qualified. They shall, except the Lieutenant Governor, reside at the seat of government during their term of office, and keep the public records, books and papers there; and shall perform such duties as may be prescribed by law.

## ARTICLE VIII.

### EDUCATION.

SECTION 1. The General Assembly shall provide a thorough and efficient system of free schools, whereby all children of this State may receive a good common school education.

§ 2. All lands, moneys, or other property, donated, granted or received for school, college, seminary or university purposes, and the proceeds threof, shall be faithfully applied to the objects for which such gifts or grants were made.

§ 3. Neither the General Assembly nor any county, city, town, township, school district, or other public corporation, shall ever make any appropriation or pay from any public fund whatever, anything in aid of any church or sectarian purpose, or to help support or sustain any school, academy, seminary. college, university, or other literary or scientific institution, controlled by any church or sectarian denomination whatever; nor shall any grant or donation of land, money or other personal property ever be made by the State or any such public corporation, to any church, or for any sectarian purpose.

§ 4. No teacher, State, county, township, or district school officer shall be interested in the sale, proceeds or profits of any book, apparatus or furniture used, or to be used, in any school in this State, with which such officer or teacher may be connected, under such penalties as may be provided by the General Assembly.

§ 5. There may be a county superintendent of schools in each county, whose qualifications, powers, duties, compensation and time and manner of election, and term of office, shall be prescribed by law.

# AN ACT

## TO ESTABLISH AND MAINTAIN A SYSTEM OF

# FREE SCHOOLS.

---

## ARTICLE I.

### STATE SUPERINTENDENT OF PUBLIC INSTRUCTION.

§ 1. Time of election and term of office. | § 4. Duties defined.
§ 2. Oath and bond. | § 5. Powers defined.
§ 3. Salary and office expenses. | § 6. Liabilities.

SECTION 1. *Be it enacted by the People of the State of Illinois, represented in the General Assembly:* That at the election to be held on Tuesday after the first Monday of November, in the year of our Lord one thousand eight hundred and ninety, and quadrennially thereafter, there shall be elected by the legal voters of this State, a State Superintendent of Public Instruction, who shall hold his office for four years from the second Monday in January next after his election, and until his successor is duly elected and qualified.

§ 2. Before entering upon his duties, he shall take and subscribe the oath of office prescribed by the constitution, and shall also execute a bond, in the penalty of twenty-five thousand dollars ($25,000). payable to the people of the State of Illinois, with securities to be approved by the Governor, conditioned for the prompt discharge of his duties as Superintendent of Public Instruction, and for the faithful application and disposition, according to law, of all school moneys that may come into his hands by virtue of his office. Said bond and oath shall be deposited with the Secretary of State, and an action may be maintained thereon by the State at any time for a breach of the conditions thereof.

§ 3. And the said State Superintendent shall receive, annually, such sum as may be provided by law, as a salary for the services required under the provisions of this act, or any other law that may be passed, and also all necessary contingent expenses for books, postage and stationery pertaining to his office, to be audited and paid by the State as the salaries and contingent expenses of other officers are paid.

§ 4. It shall be the duty of the said State Superintendent of Public Instruction—

*First*—To keep an office at the seat of government of the State.

*Second*—To file all papers, reports and public documents transmitted to him by the school officers of the several counties, each year separately.

*Third*—To keep and preserve all other public documents, books and papers relative to schools, coming into his hands as State Superintendent, and to hold the same in readiness to be exhibited to the Governor, or to any committee of either house of the General Assembly.

*Fourth*—To keep a fair record of all matters pertaining to the business of his office.

*Fifth*—To pay over, without delay, all sums of money which may come into his hands by virtue of his office, to the officer or person entitled to receive the same, in such manner as may be prescribed by law.

*Sixth*—To counsel and advise in such manner as he may deem most advisable, with experienced and practical school teachers, as to the best manner of conducting common schools.

*Seventh*—To supervise all the common and public schools in the State.

*Eighth*—To be the general adviser and assistant of county superintendents of schools in this State.

*Ninth*—To address circular letters to county superintendents, from time to time, as he shall deem for the interests of schools, giving advice as to the best manner of conducting schools, constructing school houses, furnishing the same, examining and procuring competent teachers.

*Tenth*—To, on or before the 1st day of November preceding each regular session of the General Assembly, report to the Governor the condition of the schools in the several counties of the State; the whole number of schools which have been taught in each county in each of the preceding years, commencing on the 1st of July; what part of said number have been taught by males exclusively, and what part by females exclusively; what part of the said whole number have been taught by males and females at the same time, and what part by males and females at different periods; the number of scholars in attendance at said schools; the number of persons in each county under twenty-one years of age, and the number of such persons between the ages of twelve and twenty-one years that are unable to read and write; the amount of township and county funds; the amount of the interest of the State or common school fund, and of the interests of the township and county fund annually paid out; the amount raised by an *ad valorem* tax; the whole amount annually expended for schools; the number of school houses, there kind and condition; the number of townships and parts of townships in each county; the number and description of books and apparatus purchased for the use of schools and school libraries under the provisions of this act. the price paid for the same, the total amount purchased, and what quantity and how distributed, the number and condition of the libraries, together with such other information and suggestions as he may deem important in relation to the school laws, schools, and the means of promoting education throughout the State; which report shall be laid before the General Assembly at each regular session.

*Eleventh*—To make such rules and regulations as may be necessary and expedient to carry into efficient and uniform effect the provisions of this act, and of all the laws which now are or may hereafter be in force for establishing and maintaining free schools in this State.

*Twelfth*—To be the legal adviser of all school officers, and, when requested by any such school officers, to give his opinion in writing upon any question arising under the school laws of this State.

*Thirteenth*—To hear and determine all controversies arising under the school laws of this State, coming to him by appeal from a county superintendent, upon a written statement of facts certified by the county superintendent.

*Fourteenth*—To receive and file all proper reports made to him from time to time by the several county superintendents of this State, as required by article II of this act.

*Fifteenth*—To grant State certificates to such teachers as may be found worthy to receive them, as provided for in section 2 of article VII of this act.

*Sixteenth*—To be *ex officio* a member of the board of trustees of the University of Illinois and of the Southern Normal University.

*Seventeenth*—To be *ex officio* a member of the Board of Education of the State of Illinois, and to act as secretary thereof.

*Eighteenth*—To report to the General Assembly of Illinois,. at its regular session, the condition and expenditures of the Normal University, and such other information as may be directed by the Board of Education of the State of Illinois or by the General Assembly of this State.

*Nineteenth*—To visit such of the charitable institutions of this State as are educational in their character, and to examine their facilities for instruction, and to prescribe forms for such reports as he may desire from the superintendents of such charitable institutions.

§ 5. The said State Superintendent of Public Instruction shall be clothed with the following powers—

*First*—to direct and cause the county superintendent of any county, directors or boards of trustees or township treasurer of any township, or other school officer, to withhold from any officer, township, district or teacher, any part of the common school. or township, or other school fund, until such officer, township treasurer or teacher shall have made all schedules, reports and returns required of him by this act, and until such officers shall have executed and filed all official bonds and accounted for all common school or township or other school funds which have heretofore come into his hands, as required of him by this act.

*Second*—To require the several county superintendents of this State to furnish him with such information relating to their several offices as he may desire to embody in his report to the General Assembly of this State.

*Third*—To require the board of trustees of each township in this State to make, at any time he may desire, a report similar to the report required to be made by such trustees on or before the fifteenth day of July preceding each regular session of the General Assembly of this State, as provided for in section 28 of article III of this act.

*Fourth*—Upon the recommendation of the county superintendent, or for good and sufficient reasons, to remit the forfeiture of the school fund by any township which may have failed to make the reports required by law.

*Fifth*—To determine and designate the particular statistics relating to schools which the inferior officers shall report to the county superintendent for the use of his office.

*Sixth*—To authorize the several county superintendents to procure such assistance as may be necessary to conduct county teachers' institutes for not less than.five days in each year.

*Seventh*—To require annual reports from the authorities of incorporated towns, townships, cities or districts holding schools by authority of special charters to the same extent as regular school officers are or may be required to make such reports.

*Eighth*—To require the president, principal or other proper officer of every organized university, college, seminary, academy or other literary institution, whether incorporated or unincorporated, or hereafter to be incorporated in this State. to make out such report as he may require in order that he may lay before the General Assembly a fair and full exhibit of the affairs and conditions of such institutions and of the educational resources of the State.

*Ninth*—To require the Auditor of Public Accounts to withhold from the county superintendent of any county the amount due any such county for its share of the interest on State school fund, or said county superintendent for his per diem compensation, until the report provided for in section 17 of article II of this act shall have been furnished as therein required.

§ 6. The said State Superintendent of Public Instruction shall not be interested in the sale, proceeds or profits of any book, apparatus or furniture used, or to be used, in any school in this State, and for offending against the provisions of this section he shall be liable to indictment, and upon conviction shall be fined in a sum not less than twenty-five nor more than five hundred dollars, and may be imprisoned in the county jail not less than one month nor more than twelve months, at the discretion of the court.

## ARTICLE II.

### COUNTY SUPERINTENDENTS.

| | | | |
|---|---|---|---|
| § 1. | Time of election and term of office. | § 14. | Powers defined. |
| 2. | Oath and bond. | 15. | Record of land sales. |
| 3. | Form of bond. | 16. | Report to county board. |
| 4. | Obligors bound jointly and severally. | 17. | Report to State Superintendent. |
| 5. | Supervisors may require a new bond. | 18. | Collecting statistics, and suit against trustees as individuals. |
| 6. | Office and supplies. | | |
| 7. | Liable to removal. (Repeal.) | § 19. | Approval of township treasurer's bond, and delivery of written statement to the township treasurer. |
| 8. | Vacancies. | | |
| 9. | Time limited. | | |
| 10. | Assistants. | § 20. | Apportionment of funds to townships. |
| 11. | Commissions and per diem. | 21. | Loaning of county fund. |
| 12. | Itemized bills and warrants from Auditor. | 22. | Appeal to the State Superintendent. |
| | | 23. | Delivery of money, books, papers, etc., to successor in office. |
| § 13. | Duties defined. | | |

SECTION 1. On Tuesday next after the first Monday in November, A. D., 1890, and quadrennially thereafter, there shall be elected by the qualified voters of every county in this State, a county superintendent of schools, who shall perform the duties required by law, and shall enter upon the discharge of his duties on the first Monday of December after his election.

§ 2. He shall, before entering upon his duties, take the oath prescribed by the Constitution, and execute a bond payable to the People of the State of Illinois, with two or more responsible freeholders as security, to be approved by the county board or by the judge and clerk of the county court, in a penalty of not less than twelve thousand dollars ($12,000), to be increased at the discretion of the said county board, conditioned that he will faithfully perform all the duties of his office according to the laws which are or may be in force during his term of office.

§ 3. The bond required in the foregoing section shall be in the following form, viz.:

STATE OF ILLINOIS, } ss.
............ ... .County, }

Know all men by these presents, that we, A B, C D and E F, are held and firmly bound, jointly and severally, unto the People of the State of Illinois, in the penal sum of............dollars, to the payment of which we bind ourselves, our heirs, executors and administrators firmly by these presents.

In witness whereof we have hereunto set our hands and seals this ............day of............, A. D. 18....

8

The condition of the above obligation is such, that if the above bounden A B, County Superintendent of the county aforesaid, shall faithfully discharge all the duties of such office, according to the laws which now are and may hereafter be in force, and shall deliver over to his successor in office all moneys, books, papers and property in his hands, as such County Superintendent, then this obligation to be void, otherwise to remain in full force and virtue.

A B [Seal.]
C D [Seal.]
E F [Seal.]

And which bond shall be filed in the office of the county clerk.

§ 4. The obligors in such bond shall be bound jointly and severally, and upon it an action or actions may be maintained by the board of trustees of the proper township, or any other corporate body interested, for the benefit of any township or fund injured by any breach of the conditions thereof.

§ 5. If a majority of the county board shall be satisfied, at any time, that the bond of said county superintendent is insufficient, it shall be the duty of such superintendent, upon notice being given to him by the clerk of such board, to execute a new bond, conditioned and approved as the first bond: *Provided*, that the execution of such new bond shall not affect the old bond or the liability of the securities thereon.

§ 6. It shall be the duty of the county board of the county to provide the said county superintendent with a suitable office, with necessary furniture and office supplies, as is done in the case of other county officers.

§ 7. The said county superintendent shall be liable to removal by the county board for any palpable violation of law or omission of duty. [Repealed by act approved June 15, 1893.

§ 8. When the office of county superintendent shall become vacant by death, resignation, the removal of the incumbent by the county board, or otherwise, the county board shall fill the vacancy by appointment, and the person so appointed shall hold his office until the next election of county officers, at which election the county board shall order the election of a successor.

§ 9. In counties having not more than one hundred (100) schools, the county board may limit the time of the superintendent: *Provided*, that in counties not having more than fifty (50) schools, the limit of time shall not be made less than one hundred and fifty (150) days a year; in counties having from fifty-one (51) to seventy-five (75) schools, not less than two hundred (200) days a year; and in counties having from seventy-six (76) to one hundred (100) schools, not less than two hundred and fifty (250) days a year.

§ 10. The county superintendent may, with the approval of the county board, employ such assistant or assistants as he needs for the full discharge of his duties. Such assistants shall be persons of good attainments, versed in the principles and methods of education. familiar with public school work, and competent to visit schools. Such assistants shall receive such compensation as may be fixed by the county board.

§ 11. County superintendents shall receive in full, for all services rendered by them, commissions as follows: Three per cent. commission upon the amount of sales of school lands, or sales of land upon mortgage, or of sales of real estate taken for debt, including all services therewith. Two per cent. commission upon all sums distributed, paid or loaned out by them for the support of schools. For all other duties required by law to be performed by them, four dollars ($4) a day for such number of days as shall be spent in the actual performance of their duties, not exceeding the number fixed by the county boards in counties in which the boards are given power to fix the number of days by section 9 of this article of this act, and one dollar ($1) a day for expenses for the number of days actually spent in school visitation.

§ 12. The county superintendents shall present, under oath or affirmation, their itemized bills for their per diem compensation and for the expenses allowed by this article of this act, when visiting schools, together with a report of all their acts as such county superintendent, or assistant, including a list of all the schools visited, with the dates of visitation, to the county board, at the annual meeting of such county board in September, and as near quarterly thereafter as such board may have regular or special meetings, and after the bills have been audited by the county board, the county clerk shall certify to such auditing upon the bills, and transmit them to the Auditor of Public Accounts, who shall, upon receipt of them, remit in payment thereof to each superintendent his warrant upon the State Treasurer for the amount certified to be due him. The said Auditor, in making his warrant to any county for the amount due it from the state school fund, shall deduct from it the several amounts for which warrants have been issued to the county superintendent of said county since the next preceding apportionment of the state school fund.

§ 13. It shall be the duty of each county superintendent of schools in this State—

*First*—To sell township fund lands, issue certificates of purchase, report to the county board and State Auditor, and perform all other duties pertaining thereto, as required by article XIII of this act.

*Second*—To register applicants for admission to the State Normal Universities and to the University of Illinois, and to assist in the examination of the same as directed by the State Board of Education or other proper authorities.

*Third*—To visit each school in the county at least once a year, and in the performance of this duty, he shall spend at least half the time given to his office, and more, if practicable, in visiting ungraded schools.

*Fourth*—To note, when visiting schools, the methods of instruction, the branches taught, the text-books used, and the discipline, government and general condition of the schools.

*Fifth*—To give to teachers and school officers such directions in the science, art and methods of teaching and courses of study as he may deem expedient and necessary.

*Sixth*—To act as the official adviser and constant assistant of the school officers and teachers of his county; and, in the performance of this duty, he shall faithfully carry out the advice and instruction of the State Superintendent of Public Instruction.

*Seventh*—To conduct, as provided for in section 10 of article VII of this act, a teachers' institute, and to aid and encourage the formation of other teachers' meetings, and to assist in their management.

*Eighth*—To labor in every practicable way to elevate the standard of teaching, and improve the condition of the common schools of his county.

*Ninth*—To examine, at least once each year, all books, accounts and vouchers of every township treasurer in his county, and if he finds any irregularities in them, he shall at once report the same in writing to the board of trustees, whose duty it shall be to take, immediately, such action as the case demands.

*Tenth*—To examine all notes, bonds, mortgages, and other evidences of indebtedness which the township treasurer holds officially, and if he finds that the papers are not in proper form, or that the securities are insufficient, he shall so state in writing to the board of trustees.

*Eleventh*—To give notice of the election of trustees in cases such as those provided for in section 15 of article III of this act.

*Twelfth*—To file and safely keep the poll books and returns of any election required to be returned to the county superintendent by any provision of this act.

*Thirteenth*—To investigate and determine all matters pertaining to the change in the boundaries of school districts, which may come to him by appeal from the decision of the school trustees, and to notify the township treasurer, from whom the papers relating to the matter were received, of his decision of the matter.

*Fourteenth*—To give notice of the election of school directors in cases such as are provided for in section 9 of article V of this act.

*Fifteenth*—To hold meetings, at least quarterly, for the examination of teachers, as provided for in section 7 of article VII of this act.

*Sixteenth*—To grant certificates of qualification to such persons as may be qualified to receive them, as provided for in section 3 of article VII of this act; and to keep a record of all teachers to whom such certificates have been granted, as provided for by section 4 of article VII of this act; and to keep a record of all teachers employed in teaching in his county.

*Seventeenth*—To keep a just and true account of all moneys received and all moneys paid out on account of the "institute fund," and make report thereof to the county board, as provided for in section 9 of article VII of this act.

*Eighteenth*—To present to the county board of the county. at the first regular meeting thereof, annually, the report required by section 3 of article XI of this act.

*Nineteenth*—To notify presidents of boards of trustees and clerks of school districts, on or before September 30th, annually, of the amount of money paid by him to the township treasurer, and the date of such payments.

*Twentieth*—To receive and file, on or before the 15th day of July preceding each regular session of the General Assembly, and at such other time as may be required by the State or county superintendent, a statement from the board of trustees of each township, giving such statistics and information as may be called for.

§ 14. The said county superintendent shall have power—

*First*—To require the board of trustees of each township in his county to make, at any time he may desire, the report provided for in section 28 of article III of this act.

*Second*—To recommend to the State Superintendent the remission of the penalty provided for a failure by the trustees of schools to make the reports provided for by law.

*Third*—To renew teachers' certificates at their expiration by his indorsement thereon.

*Fourth*—To revoke the certificate of any teacher for immorality, incompetency, or other just cause.

*Fifth*—To direct in what manner township treasurers shall keep their books and accounts.

*Sixth*—To bring suit against the county collector for a failure to pay State Auditor's warrant, as provided for in section 5 of article XII of this act.

*Seventh*—To remove any school director from office for a willful failure to perform the duties of his office.

*Eighth*—To lease and sell real estate in cases provided for in section 26 of article XIII of this act, in the manner therein specified.

§ 15. The said county superintendent shall provide three well bound books, which shall be paid for from the county treasury. These books shall be known and designated by the letters A, B, C for the following purposes: In book "A" he shall record at length all petitions presented to him for the sale of common school lands, and the plats and certificates of valuation made by or under the direction of the trustees of schools, and the affidavits in relation to the same. In book "B" he shall keep an account of all sales of common school lands, which account shall contain the date of sale, name of purchaser, description of land sold and the sum sold for. In book "C" he shall keep a regular account of all moneys received for lands sold or otherwise, and loaned or paid out; the persons from whom received, and on what account, and showing whether it is principal or interest; the person to whom loaned, the time for which the loan was made, the rate of interest, the names of the securities, when personal security is taken, or if real estate is taken as security, a description of the real estate; and if paid out, to whom, when, and on what account, and the amount paid out; the list of sales and the account of each township fund to be kept separate.

§ 16. The county superintendent shall report, in writing, to the county board, at their regular meeting in September of each year, giving first, the balance on hand at the time of the last report and a statement in detail of all receipts since that date, and the sources from which they were derived; second, the amount paid for expenses; third, the amount of his commissions; fourth, the amount distributed to each of the township treasurers in his county; fifth, any balance on hand. He shall also present for inspection at the same time his books and vouchers for all expenditures, and all notes or other evidences of indebtedness which he holds officially, with the securities of the same; and he shall give in writing a statement of the condition of the county fund, of the institute fund, and of any township fund of which he may have the custody.

§ 17. On or before the 15th day of August before each regular session of the General Assembly of this State, or annually, if so required by the State Superintendent of Public Instruction, the county superintendent shall communicate to said State Superintendent all such information and statistics upon the subject of schools in his said county as the said State Superintendent is bound to embody in his report to the Governor, and such other information as the State Superintendent shall require.

§ 18. In all cases where the township board of trustees of any township shall fail to prepare and forward, or cause to be prepared and forwarded to the county superintendent, the information and statistics required of them in this act, it shall be the duty of the said county superintendent to employ a competent person to take the enumeration and furnish such statistical statement, as far as practical, to the superintendent; and such person so employed shall have free access to the books and papers of said township to enable him to make such statement; and the township treasurer, or other officer or person in whose custody such books and papers may be, shall permit such person to examine such books and papers at such times and places as such person may desire for the purposes aforesaid; and the said county superintendent shall allow, and pay to the person so employed by him, for the services, such amount as he may judge reasonable out of any money which is or may come into said superintendent's hands, apportioned as the share of or belonging to such township; and the said county superintendent shall proceed to recover and collect the amount so allowed or paid for such services, in a civil action before any justice of the peace in the county, or before any court having jurisdiction, in the name of the People of the State of Illinois, of and against the trustees of schools of said township, in their individual capacity; and in such suit or suits the said county superintendent and township treasurer shall be competent witnesses; and the money so recovered, when collected, shall be paid over to the county superintendent for the benefit of said township, to replace the money taken as aforesaid.

§ 19. Whenever the bond of any township treasurer approved by the board of trustees of schools, as required by law, shall be delivered to the county superintendent, he shall carefully examine the same, and if the instrument is found in all respects to be according to law, and the securities good and sufficient, he shall endorse his approval thereon, have it recorded in the circuit clerk's office, and file the same with the papers of his office; but, if said bond is in any respect defective, or if the penalty is insufficient, he shall return it for correction. When the bond shall have been duly received and filed, the superintendent shall, on demand, deliver to said township treasurer a written statement certifying that his bond has been approved and filed, and that said township treasurer is entitled to the care and custody, on demand, of all moneys, bonds, mortgages, notes and securities, and all books, papers and property of every description belonging to said township.

§ 20. Upon the receipt of the amount due upon the Auditor's warrant, the county superintendent shall apportion said amount, also the interest on the county fund and the fines and forfeitures, to the several townships and parts of townships in his county, in which townships or parts of townships shools have been kept in accordance with the provisions of this act, and with the instructions of the State and county superintendents, according to the number of children, under twenty-one years of age, returned to him, and shall pay over the distributive share belonging to each township and fractional township, to the respective township treasurers, or other authorized person, annually: *Provided*, that no part of the State, county or other school fund shall be paid to any township treasurer or other person authorized by said treasurer, unless said township treasurer has filed his bond, as required by section 1 of article IV of this act, nor in case said treasurer is re-appointed by the trustees, unless he shall have renewed his bond and filed the same as aforesaid.

§ 21. The county superintendent may loan any money, not interest, belonging to the county fund, or to any township fund, before the same is called for, according to law, by the township treasurer, at the same rate of interest, upon the same security and for the same length of time as is provided by this act in relation to the township treasurers, and apportion the interest as provided in the preceding section; and notes and mortgages taken in the name of the "county superintendent" of the proper county are hereby declared to be as valid as if taken in the name of "trustees of schools" of the proper township, and suits may be brought in the name of "county superintendents," on all notes and mortgages heretofore or hereafter made payable to the county superintendents.

§ 22. In all controversies arising under the school law, the opinion and advice of the county superintendent shall first be sought, whence appeal may be taken to the State Superintendent of Public Instruction upon a written statement of facts certified by the county superintendent.

§ 23. The county superintendent, upon his removal or resignation, or at the expiration of his term of office (or in case of his death, his representatives) shall deliver over to his successor in office, on demand, all moneys, books, papers and personal property belonging to the office or subject to the control or disposition of the county superintendent.

## ARTICLE III.

### TOWNSHIP—TRUSTEES OF SCHOOLS.

§ 1. School township.
§ 2. Fractional townships consolidated.
§ 3. School business of the township.
§ 4. Trustees a body politic.
§ 5. Annual election.
§ 6. Term of office.
§ 7. Age, residence and eligibility.
§ 8. Notice of election, and form of election notice.
§ 9. Election in certain cases to be held on any Saturday, and notice to be given by county clerk
§ 10. Trustees draw lots for their terms of office in certain cases
§ 11. Judges of election.
§ 12. Qualifications of voters.
§ 13. Conduct of elections; contesting elections; polls may be closed at 4 p. m.
§ 14. Judges may postpone election.
§ 15. County superintendent to order election.
§ 16. Vacancies
§ 17. Tie at an election.
§ 18. More than one polling place; canvassing the returns and making out a certificate
§ 19. Election when township is same as town.
§ 20. Poll book; failure to deliver the same.
§ 21. County clerks to furnish list of trustees elected at town meetings.
§ 22. Organization; appointment of president and treasurer.
§ 23. Term of office of president and treasurer; their removal.
§ 24. Record of proceedings.
§ 25. Meetings of trustees and quorum.

§ 26. Distribution to districts; basis of the same.
§ 27. Funds placed to the credit of districts.
§ 28. Report to county superintendent; items; forfeiture for failure to report.
§ 29. Separate enumeration; statistics not divisible
§ 30. Examination of township treasurer's books, etc., by trustees.
§ 31. Gifts, grants, etc.; title of school houses.
§ 32. Sale of school house; form of notice of sale
§ 33. Conveyance of real estate; how made
§ 34. Township treasurer custodian of bonds; power to remove or sue that official.
§ 35. Power to purchase real estate in satisfaction of judgments.
§ 36. Power to make settlements.
§ 37. Power to lease land, or sell at public auction.
§ 38. Township high school, and form of notice for high school election.
§ 39. Ballots for high school election.
§ 40. Election for members of township board of education; term of office; vacancies; organization of the board, and establishment of the school.
§ 41. Powers of township board of education.
§ 42. Parts of two or more townships may join in establishing a high school.
§ 43. Discontinuance of township high school
§ 44. Canvass of ballots, and disposition of assets.
§ 45. Interests in school books; penalties.
§ 46. Districts in newly organized townships.

§ 47. Changes in district boundaries.
§ 48. Who may petition
§ 49. Districts having less than 100,000 inhabitants even under special charter, may vote to change boundaries.
§ 50. Filing of the petition; notice to the districts and form of notice.
§ 51. Territory lying in two or more townships.
§ 52. Adjournment of the board.
§ 53. Acting upon the petition
§ 54. Appeal and form of notice.
§ 55. Clerks transmit papers to the county superintendent.
§ 56. Appeal in case of territory divided by county lines.
§ 57. Filing map and list of tax-payers.

§ 58. District with a bonded debt.
§ 59. Election in new districts and form of notice
§ 60. Conduct of election.
§ 61. Organization of board.
§ 62. Election in districts organized by action of the county superintendent.
§ 63. Distribution of funds
§ 64. Appraisement of property.
§ 65. Liability of trustees in reference to distribution of funds.
§ 66. Liability of clerk.
§ 67. District failing to have school for two years
§ 68. Dissolution of union district
§ 69. Successors to trustees of school lands.

SECTION 1. Each congressional township is hereby established a township for school purposes.

§ 2. Whenever any fractional township contains less than two hundred (200) persons under twenty-one years of age, the trustees thereof, upon petition of a majority of the adult inhabitants of such fractional township, may, by written agreement entered into with the board of trustees of any adjacent township, consolidate the territory, school funds and other property of such fractional township with such adjacent township, and thereafter shall cease to exercise the functions of school trustees for such fractional township; and such territory, school funds and other property, aforesaid, shall thereafter be managed by the board of trustees of such adjacent and consolidated township, in accordance with the terms of agreement aforesaid, in the same manner as is, or may be provided by law, for the management of territory, funds and other property of school townships: *Provided*, that the said written agreement shall be duly signed by a majority of the said trustees, and filed for record by the said trustees in the office of the county clerk of the county in which such consolidated township, or the greater part thereof, is situated. [As amended June 21, 1895.

§ 3. The school business of the township shall be done by three trustees, to be elected by the legal voters of the township, as hereinafter provided for.

§ 4. Said trustees shall be a body politic and corporate, by the name and style of "trustees of schools of township No.... range No....," according to the number. The said corporation shall have perpetual existence, shall have power to sue and be sued, to plead and be impleaded in all courts and places where judicial proceedings are had.

§ 5. The election of trustees of schools shall be on the second Saturday in April, annually.

§ 6. At the first regular election of trustees, after the passage of this act, a successor to the trustee, whose term of office then expires, shall be elected, and thereafter one trustee shall be elected annually. Said trustees shall continue in office three years, and until their successors are elected and enter upon the duties of their office.

16

§ 7. No person shall be eligible to the office of trustee of schools unless twenty-one years of age, and a resident of the township. And where there are three or more school districts in any township, no two trustees shall reside, when elected, in the same school district, nor shall a person be eligible to the office of trustee of schools and school director at the same time.

§ 8. Notice of the election of school trustee shall be given by the township treasurer, upon the order of the trustees of schools,. by posting notices of such election, at least ten days previous to the time of such election, in not less than five of the most public places in said township, which notices shall specify the time and place of election and the object thereof, and may be in the following form, viz:

Public notice is hereby given that on Saturday, the............day of April, A. D......, an election will be held at.............................., between the hours of......and......of said day, for the purpose of elect-ing......school trustee for township No......, range No...... By order of the board of trustees of said township.

.............................................

*Township Treasurer.*

§ 9. In townships where no election for school trustees has heretofore been held, or in townships where, from any cause. there are no trustees of schools, the election of trustees of schools may be holden on any Saturday, notice thereof being given as required by section 8 of this article. The first election in such township shall be ordered by the county clerk of the county, who shall cause notice to be given as aforesaid.

§ 10. In case of an election held, as required by the preceding section, the trustees elected, at their first meeting, shall draw lots for their respective terms of office for one, two and three years; and thereafter one trustee shall be elected annually, at the usual time for electing trustees, to fill the vacancy occurring. At all elections after said first election, the said notice shall be given by the trustees of schools, through the township treasurer, as in other elections for trustees.

§ 11. The trustees of schools of incorporated townships present shall act as judges, and choose a person to act as clerk of said election. If the trustees (or any of them) shall fail to attend, or refuse to act when present, the legal voters present shall choose from their own number such additional judges as may be necessary. In any township lying within the limits of a city, village or incorporated town, which has adopted the provisions of "An act regulating the holding of elections, and declaring the result thereof in cities, villages and incorporated towns in this State," approved June 19, 1885, the said election

shall be held under the provisions of said act. In unincorporated townships, the qualified voters present shall choose, from
amongst themselves, the number of judges required to open
and conduct said election.

§ 12. No person shall vote at any school election held under
the provisions of this act, unless he possesses the qualifications of a voter at a general election.

§ 13. The time and manner of opening, conducting and closing said election, and the several liabilities appertaining to the
judges and clerks and to the voters, separately and collectively,
and the manner of contesting said election, shall be the same
as prescribed by the general election laws of this State defining the manner of electing magistrates and constables, so far
as applicable, subject to the provisions of this act: *Provided*,
that said election may commence, if so specified in the notice,
at any hour between the hours of eight (8) o'clock a. m., and
one (1) o'clock p. m., and the judges may close such election
at four (4) o'clock p. m.

§ 14. If, upon any day appointed for the election of trustees
of schools, the said trustees of schools or judges shall be of
opinion that, on account of the small attendance of voters, the
public good requires it, or if the majority of the voters present
shall desire it, they shall postpone said election until the next
Saturday, at the same place and hour, at which time and
meeting the voters shall proceed as if it were not a postponed
or adjourned meeting: *Provided*, that if notice shall not have
been given of such election, as required by section 8 of this
article, then and in that case said election may be ordered as
aforesaid, and holden on any other Saturday, notice thereof
being given as aforesaid.

§ 15. If the township treasurer shall fail or refuse to give
notice of the regular election of trustees, as required by said
section 8 of this article, and if, in case of a vacancy, the remaining trustee or trustees shall fail or refuse to order an election to fill such vacancy, as required by section 16 of this article, then, and in each of such cases, it shall be the duty of
the county superintendent to order an election of trustees to
fill such vacancies as aforesaid, and all elections so ordered
and held shall be valid to all intents and purposes whatever.

§ 16. When a vacancy or vacancies shall occur in the board
of trustees of schools, the remaining trustee or trustees shall
order an election to fill such vacancy, upon any Saturday,
notice to be given as required by said section 8 of this article.

§ 17. In case of a tie vote at any election of trustees of
schools, the election shall be determined by lot, on the day of
the election, by judges thereof.

§ 18. In townships where, for general elections, there are
more than two (2) polling places, the trustees shall give notice
that polls will be opened for such elections in at least two

—2 S.

places: in which case at least one of said trustees shall attend at each of said places, and additional judges shall be chosen as provided' in section eleven (11) of this article: *Provided*, there shall be at least one polling place for each eight hundred legal voters in said township. Should the polling places be in excess of the number of trustees, then the voters at such polling places so in excess shall select from their number the requisite number of voters, who shall act as judges of said election in the manner provided by said section eleven (11) for the election of trustees in unincorporated townships. Said judges shall return the ballots and original poll-books, with a certificate thereon. showing the result of the election in said precinct, to the township treasurer of the township in which said election shall be held, whereupon it shall be the duty of the board of trustees of said township, within five days after said election, to meet and to canvass the returns from each precinct. to make out a certificate showing the number of votes cast for each person in each precinct, and in the whole township, and shall file said certificate with the county superintendent of schools as otherwise provided by law.

§ 19. In counties adopting township organization, in each and every township whose boundaries coincide and are identical with those of the town, as established under the township organization laws, the trustee or trustees shall be elected at the same time and in the same manner as the town officers. In all such townships, if no trustees are elected at the stated town meeting. and when vacancies occur in the board, an election of trustee or trustees shall be ordered by the remaining trustee or trustees of schools, through the township treasurer, as provided for in section nine (9) of this article.

§ 20. Upon the election of trustees of schools, the judges of the election shall, within ten (10) days thereafter, cause a copy of the poll-book of said election to be delivered to the county superintendent of the county, with a certificate thereon showing the election of said trustees and the names of the persons elected, which copy of the poll-book, with the certificate, shall be filed by said superintendent, and shall be evidence of such election. For a failure to deliver said copy of the poll-book and certificate within the time prescribed, the judges shall be liable to a penalty of not less than twenty-five dollars ($25) nor more than one hundred dollars ($100), to be recovered in the name of the People of the State of Illinois, by action of assumpsit, before any justice of the peace of the county, which penalty. when collected, shall be added to the township school fund of the township.

§ 21. When school trustees are elected at town meetings, as provided in section nineteen (19) of this article, it shall be the duty of the county clerk. as soon as the list of the names of officers elected at the town meetings is filed with him, to give the county superintendent a list of the names of all school

19

trustees elected at the town meetings of the county, and of the towns for which they are elected.

§ 22. Within ten·days after the annual election of trustees, the board shall organize by appointing one of their number president, and some person who shall not be a director or trustee, but who shall be a resident of the township, treasurer, if there be a vacancy in this office, who shall be *ex officio* clerk of the board.

§ 23. The president shall hold his office for one year, and the treasurer for two years, and until their successors are appointed, but either of said officers may be removed by the board for good and sufficient cause.

§ 24. It shall be the duty of the president to preside at all meetings of the board and it shall be the duty of the clerk to be present at all meetings of the board, and to record in a book to be provided for the purpose all of their official proceedings, which book shall be a public record, open to the inspection of any person interested therein. All of said proceedings when recorded shall be signed by the president and clerk. If the president or clerk shall be absent or refuse to perform any of the duties of his office at any meeting of the board, a president or clerk *pro tem.* may be appointed.

§ 25. It shall be the duty of the board of trustees to hold regular semi-annual meetings on the first Mondays of April and October, and special meetings may be held at such other times as they think proper. Special meetings of the board may be called by the president or any two members thereof. At all meetings two members shall be a quorum for business.

§ 26. At the regular semi-annual meetings on the first Mondays of April and October, the trustees shall ascertain the amount of state, county and township funds on hand and subject to distribution, and shall apportion the same as follows:

*First*—Whatever sum may be due for the compensation and the books of the treasurer, and such sum as may be deemed reasonable and necessary for dividing school lands, making plats, etc.

*Second*—And the remainder of such funds shall be divided among the districts, or fractions of districts, in which schools have been kept in accordance with the provisions of this act and the instructions of the state and county superintendents during the preceding year ending June 30, in proportion to the number of children under twenty-one (21) years of age in each.

§ 27. The funds thus apportioned shall be placed on the books of the treasurer to the credit of the respective districts, and the same shall be paid out by the treasurer on the legal orders of the directors of the proper districts in the same manner as other funds of the district are paid out.

§ 28. The board of trustees of each township in this State shall prepare, or cause to be prepared, by the township treasurer, the clerk of the board, the directors of the several districts, or other person, and forwarded to the county superintendent of the county in which the township lies, on or before the 15th day of July, preceding each regular session of the General Assembly of this State, and at such other times as may be required by the county superintendent, or by the State Superintendent of Public Instruction, a statement exhibiting the condition of schools in their respective townships for the preceding biennial period, giving separately each year, commencing on the first of July and ending on the last of June, which statement shall be as follows:

*First*—The whole number of schools which have been taught in each year; what part of said number have been taught by males exclusively; what part have been taught by females exclusively; what part of said whole number have been taught by males and females at the same time, and what part by males and females at different periods.

*Second*—The whole number of scholars in attendance at all the schools, giving the number of males and females separately.

*Third*—The number of male and female teachers, giving each separately; the highest, lowest, and average monthly compensation paid to male and female teachers, giving each item separately.

*Fourth*—The number of persons under twenty-one years of age, making a separate enumeration of those above the age of twelve years who are unable to read and write, and the cause or causes of the neglect to educate them.

*Fifth*—The amount of the principal of the township fund; the amount of interest of the township fund paid into the township treasury; the amount raised by *ad valorem* tax, and the amount of such tax received into the township treasury, and amount of all other funds received into the township treasury.

*Sixth*—Amount paid for teachers' wages; the amount paid for school house lots; the amount paid for building, repairing, purchasing, renting and furnishing school houses; the amount paid for school apparatus, for books and other incidental expenses for the use of school libraries; the amount paid as compensation to township officers and others.

*Seventh*—The whole amount of the receipts and expenditures for school purposes, together with such other statistics and information in regard to schools as the State Superintendent or county superintendent may require. And any township from which such report is not received in the manner and time required by law, shall forfeit its portion of the public fund for the next ensuing year: *Provided*, that upon the recommendation of the county superintendent, or for good and sufficient reasons, the State Superintendent may remit such forfeiture.

§ 29. In all cases where a township is, or shall be divided by a county line or lines, the board of trustees of such township shall make or cause to be made separate enumerations of male and female persons of the ages as directed by section 28 of this article, designating separately the number residing in each of the counties in which such township may lie, and forward each respective number to the proper county superintendent of each of said counties; and in like manner, as far as practicable, all other statistics and information enumerated and required to be reported in the aforesaid section, shall be separately reported to the several county superintendents; and all such parts of said statistical information as are not susceptible of division and are impracticable to be reported separately, shall be reported to the county superintendent of the county in which the sixteenth section of such township is situated.

§ 30. At each semi-annual meeting, and at such other meetings as they may think proper, the said township board shall examine all books, notes, mortgages, securities, papers, moneys and effects of the corporation, and the accounts and vouchers of the township treasurer, or other township school officer, and shall make such order thereon for their security, preservation, collection, correction of errors, if any, and for their proper management, as may seem to said board necessary.

§ 31. The trustees of schools in each township in the State may receive any gift, grant, donation or devise made for the use of any school or schools, or library. or other school purposes within their jurisdiction, and they shall be and are hereby invested, in their corporate capacity. with the title, care and custody of all school houses and school house sites: *Provided*, that the supervision and control of such school houses and school house sites shall be vested in the board of directors of the district.

§ 32. When, in the opinion of any board of directors, the school house site or any buildings have become unnecessary or unsuitable or inconvenient for a school, the board of trustees, on petition of a majority of the voters of the district, shall sell and convey the same in the name of the said board, after giving at least twenty days' notice of such sale by posting up written or printed notices thereof, particularly describing said property, and the terms of sale, which notice may be in the following form, viz.:

Public notice is hereby given that on the............ day of............ A. D........, the trustees of schools of township No........, range No. ........, will sell at public sale. on the premises hereinafter described, between the hours of ten o'clock A. M., and three o clock P. M., the school house situated on the school-house site, known as (here describe the site by its number, commonly known name, or other definite description), and located in the (here describe its place in the section) which sale will be made on the following terms, to-wit: (Here insert as "one-third of the purchase money cash in hand, and the balance in two equal payments, due in one and two years from the day of sale, with interest at the rate of .... per cent. from date.")

A. B.
C. D.
E. F.
*Trustees*

And the deed of conveyance of the property so sold shall be executed by the president and clerk of said board, and the proceeds of such sale shall be paid over to the township treasurer, for the benefit of said district.

§ 33. All conveyances of real estate which may be made to said board, shall be made to said board in their corporate name, and to their successors in office.

§ 34. The township board shall cause all moneys for the use of the townships and districts, to be paid over to the township treasurer, who is hereby constituted and declared to be the only lawful depositary and custodian of all township and district school funds. They shall have power also to remove the township treasurer, at any time, for any failure or refusal to execute or comply with any order or requisition of said board, legally made and entered of record, or for other improper conduct in the discharge of his duty as treasurer. They shall also have power for any failure or refusal as aforesaid to sue him upon his official bond and recover all damages sustained by the said board in its corporate capacity, by reason of such neglect or refusal as aforesaid.

§ 35. The township trustees are hereby vested with general power and authority to purchase real estate, if in their opinion the interests of the township fund will be promoted thereby, in satisfaction of any judgment or decree wherein the said board or the county superintendent are plaintiffs or complainants; and the title of such real estate so purchased shall vest in said board for the use of the inhabitants of said township, for school purposes.

§ 36. The board of trustees are hereby vested with general power and authority to make all settlements with persons indebted to them in their official capacity; or to receive deeds to real estate in compromise; and to cancel, in such manner as they may think proper, notes, bonds, mortgages, judgments and decrees, existing or that may hereafter exist, for the benefit of the township, when the interest of said township, or of the fund concerned shall, in their opinion, require it; and their action in the premises shall be valid and binding.

§ 37. The board of trustees are hereby authorized to lease or sell at public auction, any land that may come into their possession in the manner provided for in either of the two preceding sections in such manner and on such terms as they may deem for the interests of the townships: *Provided*, that in all cases of sale of such land, the sale shall be either at the door of the court house, where judicial sales of land are usually made, or else on the premises to be sold, as the trustees may order and direct: *And, provided*, that in all cases of sale of land, as provided in this section, the sale shall be made in the manner provided for sale of the sixteenth section by section 14 of article XIII of this act.

§ 38. Upon petition of not less than fifty voters of any school township, filed with the township treasurer at least fifteen days preceding the regular election of trustees, it shall be the duty of said treasurer to notify the voters of said township that an election "For" or "Against" a township high school will be held at the said next regular election of trustees, by posting notices of such election in at least ten of the most public places throughout such township, for at least ten days before the day of such regular election; which notices may be in the following form, viz.:

### "HIGH SCHOOL ELECTION."

Notice is hereby given that on Saturday, the............day of April, A. D..............., an election will be held at....................for the purpose of voting "For" or "Against" the proposition to establish a township high school for the benefit of township No........, range No....... The polls for said election will be open at.........and close at......... o'clock of said day.

A. B.,
*Township Treasurer.*

*Provided,* that when any city in this State, having a population of not less than one thousand and not over one hundred thousand inhabitants, lies within two or more townships, then that township in which a majority of the inhabitants of said city reside shall, together with said city, constitute a school township under this act for high school purposes. [As amended by act approved June 19, 1891.

§ 39. The ballots for such election shall be received and canvassed as in other elections, and may have thereon the name of the person or persons whom the voter desires for trustee or trustees.

§ 40. If a majority of the votes at such election shall be found to be in favor of establishing a township high school, it shall be the duty of the trustees of the township to call a special election on any Saturday within sixty days from the time of the election establishing the township high school, for the purpose of electing a township board of education, to consist of five members, notice of which election shall be given for the same time and in the same manner as provided for in the election of township trustees. The members elected shall determine by lot, at their first meeting, the length of term each is to serve. Two of the members shall serve for one year each, two for two years, and one for three years, from the second Saturday of April next preceding their election. Whenever a vacancy occurs (except by death or resignation), a successor or successors shall be elected, each of whom shall serve for three years, which subsequent election shall be held on the same day and in the same manner as the election of township trustees. In case of vacancy from other cause than the expiration of the term of office, the board shall call an election without delay, which election may be held on any Saturday, notice of which shall be given for the same time and in the same manner as for the election of township trustees. Within ten days after their election, the members of the township board of education shall meet and organize by electing one of their number president, and by electing a secretary. It shall be the duty of the township board of education to establish at some central point most convenient to a majority of the pupils of the township, a high school for the education of the more advanced pupils.

§ 41. For the purpose of building a school house, supporting the school and paying other necessary expenses, the town-. ship shall be regarded as a school district; and the township board of education shall have the power and discharge the duties of directors for such district in all respects.

§ 42. In like manner the voters and trustees of two or more adjoining townships, or parts of townships, may co-operate in the establishment and maintenance of a high school, on such terms as they may, by written agreement made and signed by the boards of trustees, enter into.

§ 43. When any township, townships or parts of townships shall have organized a high school, and wish to discontinue the same, upon petition of not less than a majority of the legal voters of said township, townships or parts of townships, filed with the township treasurers of said townships at least fifteen days preceding a regular election of trustees, it shall be the duty of the said treasurers to notify the voters of the township, townships or parts of townships, that an election will be held on the day of said regular election of trustees, for the purpose of voting "For" or "Against" discontinuing the township high school; which notice shall be given in the same manner and for the same length of time, and may be in substantially the same form as the notice provided for in section 38 of this article.

§ 44. The ballots for such election shall be received and canvassed in the same manner as provided for in section 39 of this article. If the majority of the votes at such election shall be found in favor of discontinuing the high school, it shall be the duty of the trustees to discontinue the same, and turn all the assets of the said high school over to the school fund of the township or townships interested therein, in proportion to the assessed valuation of said townships, to be used as any other township fund for school purposes.

§ 45. No trustee of schools shall be interested in the sales, proceeds or profits of any book, apparatus or furniture used in any school in this State with which such trustee may be in any manner connected. For offending against the provisions of this section, any such trustee shall be liable to indictment, and, upon conviction, shall be fined in a sum not less than twenty-five dollars nor more than five hundred dollars, and may be imprisoned in the county jail not less than one nor more than twelve months, at the discretion of the court.

§ 46. Trustees of schools in newly organized townships shall lay off the township into one or more school districts, to suit the wishes or convenience of a majority of the inhabitants of the township, and shall prepare or cause to be prepared a map of the the township, on which map shall be designated the district or districts, to be styled, when there are more districts than one, "District No. ...., in township No. ...., range No. ...., of the .... P. M. (according to the proper numbers), county of ............, and State of Illinois."

§ 47. In a township where such division into districts has been made, the said trustees may, in their discretion, at the regular meeting in April. when petitioned as hereinafter provided for, change such districts as lie wholly within their township, so as—

*First*—To divide or consolidate districts.

*Second*—To organize a new district out of territory belonging to two or more districts.

*Third*—To detach territory from one district and add the same to another district adjacent thereto.

§ 48. No change shall be made as provided for in the preceding section, unless petitioned for—

*First*—By a majority of the legal voters of each of the districts affected by the proposed change.

*Second*—By two-thirds (⅔) of the legal voters living within certain territory, described in the petition, asking that said territory be detached from one district and added to another.

*Third*—By two-thirds (⅔) of all the legal voters living within certain territory, containing not less than ten (10) families, asking that said territory may be made a new district.

§ 49. In school districts having a population of not less than one thousand inhabitants, whether acting under the general school law or organized and acting under a special charter, desiring a change of boundaries, the question of such change may be submitted to the trustees by a vote of the people, instead of by the petition provided for in the preceding section; and when petitioned so to do by twenty-five legal voters of the district, the school board of the district shall submit the question of the change desired to the voters of said district, at a special election called for that purpose, and held at least thirty days prior to the regular April meeting of trustees. If a majority of the votes cast at any such election shall be in favor of the change proposed, then, due return of the election having been made to the township treasurer, the township trustees shall consider and take action the same as if petitioned therefor by a majority of the legal voters of such district: *Provided*, that no question of change of boundaries shall be submitted to a vote of the school district more than once in any year. [As amended by act approved June 18, 1891].

§ 50. No petition shall be acted upon by the board of trustees unless such petition shall have been filed with the clerk of the said board of trustees at least twenty days before the regular meeting in April, nor unless a copy of the petition, together with a notice in writing, signed by one or more of the petitioners, shall be delivered by the petitioners, or some one of them, at least ten days before the date at which the petition is to be considered, . to the president or clerk of the board of directors of each district whose boundaries will be changed if the petition is granted.

Which notice may be in the following form, to-wit:

The directors in District No. ...., in township No. ...., range No. ....
of the .... principal meridian, will take notice that the undersigned and
others have made and filed with the board of trustees of said township
their petition. a copy of which is herewith handed to you.
                Signed.....................................

§ 51. At the said April meeting, by the concurrent action of the several boards of trustees of the townships in which the district or districts affected lie, each board being petitioned as provided for in section 48 of this article, the same changes may be made in the boundaries both of districts which lie in separate townships, but adjacent to each other, and of districts formed of parts of two or more townships, as are permitted to be made in districts which lie wholly in one township.

§ 52. When, at the regular meeting of the trustees in April, any petition shall come before the trustees, asking for any change in boundaries, it shall be the duty of the trustees to ascertain if the foregoing provisions have been strictly complied with; and if it shall appear that they, or either of them, have not been complied with, then, in such case, the board shall adjourn for not longer than four weeks, in order that the foregoing provisions may be complied with, but there shall be but one adjournment for such purpose.

§ 53. If, on the day of the regular meeting, or. in case of an adjournment, at the adjourned meeting, it shall appear that such provisions have been complied with, then the trustees shall consider the petition, and shall also hear any legal voters living in the district or districts that will be affected by the change if made, who may appear before them to oppose the petition, and they shall grant or refuse the prayer of the petitioners without unreasonable delay. After the trustees shall consider the petition, no objection shall be thereafter raised as to its form, and their action shall be *prima facie* evidence that all the formal requirements have been complied with.

§ 54. The petitioners, or the legal voters who nave appeared before the trustees at the meeting when the petition was considered, and opposed the same, shall have the right of appeal to the county superintendent of schools: *Provided*, that the party appealing files with the clerk of the trustees a written notice of appeal within ten days after the final action upon the petition by the trustees, which notice may be in the following form, to-wit:

To the trustees of schools, township No. ....., range No.... of.........
county, Illinois:

You are hereby notified that the undersigned will appeal from your decision. made on the......day of............, A. D........., granting (or refusing) the prayer of the petition in regard to (here give substance of the petition concerned) to the county superintendent of schools of.......
county, Illinois, as provided by law.

Signed..............................

§ 55. When an appeal is taken from the action of the trustees to the county superintendent, the clerk of the trustees shall, within five days after the written notice of the appeal has been filed with him by the appellants, transmit all the papers in the case, with a transcript of the records of the trustees, showing their action thereon to the county superintendent; and, in case of an appeal, the township treasurer shall be required to take no further action in the matter, except upon the order of the county superintendent, whose duty it shall be to investigate the case upon such appeal; and if, in his opinion, the change asked is for the best interest of the district or districts concerned, he shall make such change or changes, but if he considers the proposed change unadvisable, he shall refuse to make it, and shall reverse, if need be, the action of the trustees, and shall give the clerk, from whom he received the paper, immediate notice of his decision; and his action shall be final and binding. If the changes asked for by the petitioners shall be made by the county superintendent, he shall notify, in writing, the clerk by whom the papers in the case were transmitted to him, of his action, and the clerk shall thereupon make a record of the same, and shall, within ten days thereafter, make a copy of the same, and a map of the township, showing the districts, and an accurate list of the tax-payers of the newly arranged districts, and deliver them to the county clerk for filing and record by him, the same as if the changes had been ordered by the trustees.

§ 56. In all cases where the territory affected by a proposed change of district boundaries is divided by a county line or lines, the appeal may be taken to the county superintendent of schools of any one of the counties in which said territory is partly located; and upon any appeal being taken in any such case, the county superintendent of schools, to whom such appeal is taken, shall forthwith, give notice to the county superintendent or superintendents of schools of the other county or counties, of the pendency of such appeal, and of the time and place when and where it will be heard; and the county superintendents of schools of the counties in which the said territory is located, shall meet together at such time and place, and together hear

and determine said appeal. In case the said county superintendents shall be unable to arrive at an agreement, then the
county judge of the county where such appeal is pending shall
be called, and shall constitute one of the board of appeal, and
thereupon the appeal shall be heard and determined by them.
And the county superintendent of schools to whom such appeal
is taken shall at once notify, in writing, the clerk by whom
the papers in the case were transmitted to him of the action
taken on such appeal, as hereinafter provided.

§ 57. Whenever change in boundaries is made by the trustees of schools, if no appeal is taken to the county superintendent, the clerk of the trustees shall make a complete copy
of the record of the action of the trustees; which copy shall
be certified by the president of the trustees and the clerk who
shall file the same, together with a map of the township, showing the districts, and an accurate list of the tax-payers of the
newly arranged districts, with the county clerk for record
within twenty days of the action of the trustees.

§ 58. In case any territory shall be set off from any district that has a bonded debt, the change not being petitioned
for by a majority of the legal voters of said district, such
original district shall remain liable for the payment of such
bonded debt as if not divided. The directors of the original
district having such bonded debt and of the district into which
the territory taken from such original district has been incorporated or formed, shall constitute a joint board for the purpose of determining and certifying, and they shall determine
and certify to the county clerk the amount of tax required
yearly for the purpose of paying the interest and principal of
such bonded debt; which tax shall be extended by the county
clerk against all property embraced within such original district as if it had not been divided.

§ 59. When the trustees of schools shall organize a new district, as hereinbefore provided for, it shall be the duty of the
clerk of the board of trustees, if no appeal is taken to the
county superintendent, to order, within fifteen days after the
action of the trustees, an election, to be held at some convenient time and place, within the boundaries of such newly organized district, for the election of three school directors, notice
being given by the township treasurer, who shall post up at
least three notices of such election in at least three prominent
places in said district, at least ten days prior to the time appointed for holding such election, which notices shall specify
the place where such election is to be held, the time for opening and closing the polls, and the object of said election,
which notice may be in the following form, to-wit:

"ELECTION NOTICE."

Public notice is hereby given that on the........day of............A. D.
......an election will be held at...............for the purpose of electing
three school directors for the new district known as district No....., in
township No......, range No......, of the......P. M., in..........county,
Illinois.

The polls at said election will be open at.....o'clock......M., and close
at......o'clock....M.
By order of the board of trustees of said township.

Signed..........................
*Township Treasurer.*

§ 60. At the time appointed for opening the polls for said
election, it shall be the duty of the legal voters present, five of
whom shall constitute a quorum, to appoint three of their
number, two of whom shall act as judges, and one as clerk of
said election; and the election in all other respects shall be conducted as other elections for the election of school directors.

§ 61. Within ten days after the election, it shall be the duty
of the directors, elected at such election, to meet at some convenient time and place previously agreed upon by said directors, and organize as a district board by appointing one of
their number president, and another of their number clerk of
said board, as in other cases of the election of school directors.
At this first meeting of the directors, they shall draw lots for
their respective terms of office for one, two and three years,
each of which shall be considered a fractional term, ending at
each annual meeting according to the term drawn.

§ 62. In case a new district is organized by the action of
the county superintendent, the said clerk of the board of trustees shall, within five days after he has received notice of the
action of the county superintendent on the appeal, order an
election of directors in the new district, the same as if the
change had been made by the board of trustees, and such election shall be held in the same manner as the election provided
for where the trustees have formed such new district.

§ 63. Whenever a new district has been formed by the trustees, or by the county superintendent, or county superintendents, from a part of a district or from parts of two or more
districts, the trustees of the township or townships concerned
shall proceed forthwith to make a distribution of tax funds, or
other funds which are in the hands of the treasurer, or to which
the district may, at the time of such division, be entitled; so
that both the old and new districts shall receive parts of such
funds, in proportion to the amount of taxes collected next preceding such division from the taxable property in the territory
composing the several districts. If the new district be composed
of parts of two or more districts, the trustees shall make distribution of said funds between the new district and the old
districts, respectively, so that the new district shall receive a
distribution of the funds of each of the old districts, in the
proportion which the amount of taxes collected from the prop-

erty in the territory of the new district bears to the whole taxes collected, next before the division, in the old district; and the town treasurer shall forthwith place the sum so distributed to the credit of the respective districts, and shall immediately place the proportion of the funds to which said new district may be entitled to its credit on his books, and the funds on hand shall be subject at once to the order of the directors of the new district, and those not on hand as soon as collected.

§ 64. The trustees of the township or townships concerned shall, at the time of the creation of a new district, or within the period of thirty days thereafter, proceed to the appointment of three appraisers, who shall not be citizens of the township or townships interested. It shall be the duty of said appraisers, within thirty days after their appointment, to appraise the school property, both real and personal, of the district or districts interested, at their fair cash value. Within thirty days after such appraisement, the trustee or trustees of the township or townships concerned shall proceed to charge the property to the district in which it may be found, and to credit the other district interested therein with its proportion of such valuation: *Provided*, that the *bona fide* debts, if any, of the old district, shall first be deducted and the balance charged and credited as aforesaid and the trustees shall direct the treasurer to place to the credit of the district not retaining said property, its proportion of the value of said property, and of the funds then on hand, or subsequently to accrue, belonging to such district to which such property is charged.

§ 65. If the trustees shall fail to observe the provisions of sections 63 and 64, in reference to distribution of funds and property, they shall be individually and jointly liable to the district interested, in an action on the case, to the full amount of the damages sustained by the district aggrieved. Where trustees have heretofore failed to make distribution of property to districts, as provided in said sections 63 and 64 of this article, the district interested in the making of such distribution may, by its directors, request the trustees, in writing, to proceed to make such distribution; and said trustees shall proceed to make such distribution in the manner prescribed, and shall be liable, as herein stated, for a neglect or failure so to do.

§ 66. The clerk of any board of trustees who shall fail, neglect, or refuse to perform the duties imposed upon him by this article of this act, or any of them, within the time and in the manner prescribed, shall, for each offense, forfeit not less than ten dollars ($10), nor more than twenty-five dollars ($25) of his pay as clerk of the board of trustees and township treasurer, which forfeiture shall be enforced by the trustees.

§ 67. If any school district shall, for two consecutive years, fail to maintain a public school, as required by law to do, it shall be the duty of the trustees of schools of the township, or townships, in which such district lies, to attach the territory of such district to one or more adjoining school districts; and, in case said territory is added to two or more districts, to divide the property of said district between the districts to which its territory is added, in the manner hereinbefore provided for the division of property in case a new district is organized from a part of another district, and the action of the trustees in such a case shall be final and binding. And the clerk of the trustees in such case shall file a copy of the record of the same, together with the map and list of tax-payers with the county clerk as in other cases of change of district boundaries.

§ 68. The majority of legal voters of a district lying in two or more townships may secure the dissolution of said district by petitioning the several boards of trustees of said townships, at their regular meeting in April, that each will add the territory belonging to said district, in its township, to one or more adjacent districts. Upon receipt of such petition, or the returns of the election (in districts containing one thousand or more inhabitants) the several boards of trustees shall each make such disposition of the territory of said district as lies in its township, and they shall jointly make such division of property of said district between the districts to which its territory is attached, as is hereinbefore provided in the case of the organization of a new district from a part of another district. The action of the trustees, in accordance with such petition or election, shall be final and binding; and the clerks of the several boards of trustees. in such case, shall file a copy of the record of the same, together with the map and lists of tax-payers, with the county clerk, as in other cases of change of district boundaries.

§ 69. The trustees of schools, elected as provided for in this article, shall be the successors to the trustees of school lands, appointed by the county commissioners' court, and of trustees of schools elected in townships under the provisions of "An act making provisions for organizing and maintaining common schools," approved February 26, 1841, and "An act to establish and maintain common schools," approved March 1, 1847, and "An act to establish and maintain a system of free schools," approved April 1, 1872. All rights of property, and rights and causes of action, existing or vested in the trustees of school lands, or the trustees of schools appointed or elected as aforesaid, for the use of the inhabitants of the township, or any part of them, shall vest in the trustees of schools, as successors, in as full and complete a manner as was vested in the trustees of school lands, or the trustees of schools appointed and elected as aforesaid.

# ARTICLE IV.

## TOWNSHIP TREASURER.

§ 1. Bond; form of bond.
§ 2. Treasurer's accounts; record of notes and bonds; subject to inspection.
§ 3. Terms of loans.
§ 4. Securities to run to board of trustees.
§ 5. Surplus district funds may be loaned.
§ 6. Statement of loans to be delivered to county superintendent.
§ 7. Form and release of mortgage.
§ 8. Action on mortgage; insurance policies.
§ 9. Additional security.
§ 10. Preference given to debts due to school fund.
§ 11. Default in payment; penalty; action to recover interest.
§ 12. Manner of bringing suits.

§ 13. Treasurer shall keep money, books and papers, and keep funds at interest.
§ 14. Send annual statement to trustees.
§ 15. Annual exhibit.
§ 16. Statement to districts; exhibit to be posted.
§ 17. Penalty for failure to perform requirements of the preceding sections.
§ 18. Unpaid orders of teachers to draw interest.
§ 19. Additional duties defined .
§ 20. Treasurer liable for failure to perform his duties, but not liable when acting under orders of board.
§ 21. Bonds, securities, etc., to be turned over to successor; penalty and judgment.
§ 22. Compensation of the treasurer.

§ 1. The township treasurer appointed by the board of trustees of schools shall, before entering upon his duties, execute a bond with two or more freeholders, who shall not be members of the board, as securities, payable to the board of trustees of the township for which he is appointed treasurer, with a sufficient penalty to cover all liabilities which may be incurred, conditioned faithfully to perform all the duties of township treasurer in township No........., range No........, in...... county according to law; which bond shall be approved by at least a majority of the board, and shall be delivered by one of the trustees to the county superintendent of the proper county. And in all cases where such treasurer aforesaid is to have the custody of all bonds, mortgages, moneys and effects denominated principal, and belonging to the township for which he is appointed treasurer, the penalty of said treasurer's bonds shall be twice the amount of all bonds, notes, mortgages, moneys and effects; and shall provide for the faithful accounting for, and turning over, of all such bonds, notes, mortgages, moneys and effects as shall come into his hands while he may act as such treasurer, under such appointment, to his successor, when appointed and qualified, as herein provided, by giving bond. The penalty of said bond shall be increased from time to time, as the increase of the amount of notes, bonds, mortgages and effects may require, and whenever, in the judgment of the trustees or county superintendent, the security is insufficient. Any and every township treasurer appointed subsequent to the first, as herein provided, shall execute bond with security, as is required of the first treasurer.

The bond required in this section shall be in the following form, viz.:

STATE OF ILLINOIS, } ss.
.......... County, }

Know all men by these presents, that we, A. B., C. D. and E. F., are held and firmly bound, jointly and severally, unto the board of trustees of township.........., range.........., in said county, in the penal sum of ..............dollars, for the payment of which we bind ourselves, our heirs, executors and administrators firmly by these presents.

In witness whereof we have hereunto set our hands and seals this..... day of ............, A. D., 18.... The condition of the above obligation is such that if the above bounden A. B., township treasurer of township ............, range ............, in the county aforesaid, shall faithfully discharge the duties of said office, according to the laws which now are or may hereafter be in force, and shall deliver to his successor in office, after such successor shall have fully qualified by giving bond as provided by law, all moneys, books, papers, securities and property which shall come into his hands or control, as such township treasurer, from the date of this bond up to the time that his successor shall have duly qualified as township treasurer, by giving such bond as shall be required by law, then this obligation to be void; otherwise to remain in full force and virtue.

Approved and accepted by:

G. H., }
I. J.,  } Trustees.
K. L., }

A. B., (Seal.)
C. D., (Seal.)
E. F. (Seal.)

§ 2. Every township treasurer shall provide himself with two well bound books, the one to be called a cash book, the other a loan book. He shall charge himself in the cash book with all moneys received, stating the charge, when, from whom, and on what account received, and credit himself with all moneys paid or loaned, stating the amount loaned, the date of the loan, the rate of interest, the time when payable, the name of the securities; or, if real estate to be taken, a description of the same.

He shall also enter, in separate accounts, moneys received and moneys paid out, charging the first to debit account, and crediting the latter as follows, to-wit:

*First*—The principal of the township fund, when paid in and when paid out.

*Second*—The interest of the township fund, when received and when paid out.

*Third*—The common school fund and other funds, when received from the county superintendent and when paid out.

*Fourth*—The taxes received from the county or town collector, for what district received, and when and for what purpose paid out.

*Fifth*—Donations received.

*Sixth*—Moneys coming from all other sources; and in all cases entering the date when received, and when paid out. And he shall also arrange and keep his books and accounts in such other manner as may be directed by the State or county superintendent or the board of trustees. He shall also provide a book, to be called a journal, in which he shall record, fully and at length, the acts and proceedings of the board, their

orders, by-laws and resolutions. And he shall also provide a
book, to be called a record, in which he shall enter a brief description of all notes or bonds belonging to the township, and
upon the opposite page he shall note down when paid, or any
remarks to show where or in what condition it is, as in the
following form, viz. :

| Maker's Name. | Date of Note. | When Due. | Amount. | Remarks. |
|---|---|---|---|---|
| A. B., C. D., E. F. | January 1, 18.. | January 1, 18.. | $90.00 | January 6, 18..., handed to I. J., for collection. or January 6, 18.., paid. |

All the books and accounts of the treasurer shall at all times
be subject to the inspection of the trustees, directors or other
person authorized by this act, or by any committee appointed
by the voters of the township, at the annual election of trustees, to examine the same.

§ 3. Township treasurers shall loan, upon the following conditions, all moneys which shall come to their hands by virtue of
their office, except such as may be subject to distribution. The
rate of interest shall not be less than six (6) per cent., nor
more than eight (8) per cent. per annum,* payable annually,
the rate of interest to be determined by a majority of the township trustees at any regular or special meeting of their board.
No loans shall be made for less than six (6) months, nor more
than five (5) years. For all sums not exceeding two hundred
dollars ($200) loaned for not more than one year, two (2) re-
sponsible sureties shall be given; for all sums over two hundred
dollars ($200), and for all loans for more than one (1) year,
security shall be given by mortgage on real estate unincum-
bered, in value forty per cent. more than the amount loaned,
with a condition that in case additional security shall be at any
time required, the same shall be given to the satisfaction of the
board of trustees for the time being: *Provided,* that nothing
herein shall prevent the loaning of township funds to boards of
school directors, taking bonds therefor, as provided in section
1, article IX, of this act.

§ 4. Notes, bonds, mortgages and other securities taken for
money or other property due, or to become due to the board
of trustees for the township, shall be payable to the said board
by their corporate name; and in such name, suits, actions and
complaints, and every description of legal proceedings may be
had for the recovery of money, the breach of contracts and for
every legal liability which may at any time arise or exist, or
upon which a right of action shall accrue to the use of such corporation: *Provided, however,* that notes, bonds, mortgages
and other securities in which the name of the county superintendent, or of the trustees of schools are inserted, shall be valid

* 7 per cent. is the highest rate allowed by law on loans made on or after July 1, 1891.

to all intents and purposes; and suit shall be brought in the name of the board of trustees as aforesaid. The wife of the mortgagor (if he is married) shall join in the mortgage given to secure the payment of money loaned by virtue of the provisions of this act.

§ 5. Whenever there is a surplus fund in the treasurer's hands belonging to any school district, the treasurer may loan the same for the use and benefit of such district, upon the written request of the directors of said district and not otherwise; and all such loans shall be on the same conditions as are prescribed in this article for the loaning of township funds.

§ 6. The township treasurer shall, on or before the 30th day of June, annually, prepare and deliver to the county superintendent of his county, a statement, verified by his affidavit, showing the exact condition of the township funds. Said statement shall contain a description of the securities, bonds, mortgages and notes belonging to the township, giving names of securities, dates, amount of loans, rate of interest, when due, and all data by which a full understanding of the condition of the funds may be obtained. The county superintendent shall preserve such statement for the use of the township.

§ 7. Mortgages to secure the payment of money loaned under the provisions of this act, may be in the following form, viz.:

I, A. B., of the county of .............., and State of............, do hereby grant, convey and transfer to the trustees of school of township ............, range No............., in the county of.........., and State of Illinois, for the use of the inhabitants of said township, the following described real estate, to-wit: (Here insert premises), which real estate I declare to be in mortgage for the payment of............dollars loaned to me, and for the payment of all interest that may accrue thereon to be computed at the rate of.........per cent. per annum until paid. And I do hereby covenant to pay the said sum of money in..........years from the date hereof, and to pay the interest on the same annually, at the rate aforesaid. I further covenant that I have a good and valid title to said estate, and that the same is free from all incumbrance, and that I will pay all taxes and assessments which may be levied on said estate, and that I will give any additional security that may at any time be required in writing by said board of trustees; and if said estate be sold to pay said debt, or any part thereof, or for any failure or refusal to comply with or perform the conditions of covenant herein contained, I will deliver immediate possession of the premises. And it is further agreed, by and between the parties, in case a bill is filed in any court to foreclose this mortgage for non-payment of either principal or interest, that the mortgagor will pay a reasonable solicitor's fee, and the same shall be included in the decree and be taxed as costs: and we, A. B., and C., wife of A. B., hereby release all right to the said premises which we may have by virtue of any homestead laws of this State, and in consideration of the premises, C., wife of A. B., doth hereby release to said board all her right and title of dower in the aforegranted premises for the purpose aforesaid.

In testimony whereof, we have hereby set our hands and seals this ................day of..................., 18....

A. B. (Seal.)
C. B. (Seal.)

Which mortgage shall be acknowledged and recorded as is required by law for other conveyances of . real estate, the mortgagor paying expenses of acknowledgment and recording.

On payment of any school mortgage in full, it shall be the duty of the trustees of schools to give a deed of release of such mortgage or to enter satisfaction thereof upon the record, such deed of release or satisfaction to be executed by the township treasurer.

§ 8. Upon the breach of any condition or stipulation contained in said mortgage, an action may be maintained and damages recovered as upon other covenants; but mortgages made in any other form to secure payment, as aforesaid, shall be valid as if no form had been prescribed. In estimating the value of real estate mortgaged to secure the payment of money loaned under the provisions of this law, the value of improvements liable to be destroyed may be included; but in any such case said improvements shall be insured for the insurable value thereof in some safe and responsible insurance company or companies, and the policy or policies of insurance shall be transferable to the board of trustees as additional security for any loan, and shall be kept so insured until the loan is paid.

§ 9. In all cases where the board of trustees shall require additional security for the payment of money loaned, and such security shall not be given, the township treasurer shall cause suit to be instituted for the recovery of the same, and all interest thereon to the date of judgment: *Provided*, that proof be made of the said requisition.

§ 10. In the payment of debts by executors and administrators, those due the common school or township fund shall have a preference over all other debts, except funeral expenses, the widows award, and the expenses attending the last sickness. not including the physician's bill. And it shall be the duty of the township treasurer to attend at the office of the probate judge upon the proper day, as other creditors, and have any debts, as aforesaid, probated and classed, to be paid as aforesaid.

§ 11. If default be made in the payment of interest due upon money loaned by any county superintendent or township treasurer, or in the payment of the principal, interest at the rate of twelve per cent. per annum shall be charged upon the principal and interest from the day of default, which interest shall be included in the assessment of damages; or in the judgment in the suit or action brought upon the obligation to enforce payment thereof, and interest as aforesaid may be recovered in an action brought to recover interest only. The said township treasurer is hereby empowered to bring appropriate actions in the name of the board of trustees, for the recovery of the yearly interest, when due and unpaid, without suing for the principal, in whatever form secured; and justices of the peace shall have jurisdiction of such cases of all sums not exceeding two hundred dollars.

§ 12. All suits brought or actions instituted under the provisions of this act, may be brought in the name of the trustees of schools of township No. ...., range No. ...., except as provided for *qui tam* actions, or actions in favor of county superintendents.

§ 13. The said township treasurer shall demand, receive and safely keep, according to law, all moneys, books and papers of every description belonging to his township. He shall keep the township funds loaned at interest; and if, on the first Monday in October, in any year, there shall be any interest or other funds on hand which shall not be required for distribution, such amount not required as aforesaid, may, if the board of trustees see proper, forever be considered as principal in the funds to which it belongs, and loaned as such.

§ 14. On the first Mondays in April and October of every year, the township treasurer shall lay before the board of trustees a statement showing the amount of interest, rents, issues and profits that have accrued or become due since their last regular half-yearly meeting, on the township lands and township funds, and also the amount of state and county fund interest on hand. He shall also lay before the said trustees all books, notes, bonds, mortgages and all other evidences of indebtedness belonging to the township, for the examination of the trustees; and shall make such other statement as the board may require, touching the duties of his office.

§ 15. The said township treasurer shall make out annually, and present io the board of trustees, at their meeting succeeding the annual election, a complete exhibit of the fiscal affairs of the township, and of the several districts or parts of districts in the township, showing the receipts of money, and the sources from which they have been derived, and the deficit and delinquencies, if there be any, and the cause, as well as a classified statement of moneys paid out, and the amount of obligations remaining unpaid.

§ 16. The township treasurer shall, within two days after the first Monday in April, and on July fifteenth in each year, make out for each district or part of district in the township, a statement or exhibit of the exact condition of the account of such district or part of district, as shown by his books on April first and June thirtieth of each year; which statement or exhibit shall show the balance at the time of making the last exhibit, and the amount received since, up to the time of making the exhibit, and when and from what source received; and it shall also show the amount paid out during the same time, to whom paid, and for what purpose, and shall be balanced, and the balance shown. It shall be the duty of said treasurer to comply with any lawful demand the said trustees may make as to the verification of any balance reported by said treasurer to be on hand. The exhibit shall be subscribed and sworn to by the treasurer before any officer authorized to administer an oath, and shall then, by the treasurer, be, without delay, delivered or transmitted by mail to the clerk of the board of directors of the proper district. It shall be the duty of the said clerk, upon receiving such exhibit, to enter the same upon the records of the district, and, at the next annual election of directors thereafter, to cause a copy thereof to be posted up at the front door of the building where such election is held.

§ 17. For a failure on the part of the treasurer, clerk of any board of directors, or any director, to comply with any of the requirements of the preceding sections of this article, he shall be liable to a penalty of not less than five dollars ($5) nor more than fifty dollars ($50), to be recovered before any justice of the peace of the county in which the offense is committed.

§ 18. When any order drawn for the payment of a teacher, is presented to the township treasurer for payment, and is not paid for want of funds, the said treasurer shall make a written statement over his signature by an endorsement on such order, with date, showing such presentation and non-payment, and shall make and keep a record of such endorsement. Such order shall thereafter draw interest at the rate of eight per cent. per annum until paid, or until the treasurer shall, in writing, notify the clerk of the board of directors that he has funds to pay such order; and of said notice, the said treasurer shall make and keep a record; after giving said notice, he shall hold the funds necessary to pay such order until it is presented for payment, and such order shall draw no interest after the giving of said notice to said clerk of the board.

§ 19. In addition to the foregoing requirements, it shall be the duty of the said township treasurer—

*First*—To return to the county clerk of his county, on or before the second Monday in August in each year, the certificate of tax levy made by each board of school directors in his township.

*Second*—To pay, whenever he has funds in his hands belonging to the district, all lawful orders drawn on him by the board of directors of any school district in his township.

*Third*—To collect, from the collector of taxes of the township and the county collector of taxes, the full amount of the tax levies made by the several boards of directors in his township.

*Fourth*—To examine the official record of each school district in the township on the first Mondays in April and October of each year.

*Fifth*—To keep a correct account between the districts where pupils are transferred by the directors from one district to another.

*Sixth*—To give, upon the order of the trustees of schools, notice of the election of trustees, as required by law.

*Seventh*—To give, in case of the formation of a new school district, notice of the election of a board of school directors.

*Eighth*—To cause to be published in some newspaper published in his county an annual statement of the finances of the township, as required by law.

*Ninth*—To make, whenever a change has been made in the boundaries of a school district, a complete copy of the records of the trustees, a map of the township showing such change of boundaries, and an accurate list of the tax-payers in the newly arranged districts, and file the same with the county clerk within twenty days of the time such change was made.

*Tenth*—To file and safely keep all poll-books and returns of elections which may be delivered to him under any provisions of this act.

*Eleventh*—To receive and safely keep all moneys, sucurities, papers and effects belonging to the township or the school districts, which, by law, are required to be deposited with such treasurer.

§ 20. For any failure or refusal to perform all the duties required of the township treasurer by law, he shall be liable to the board of trustees, upon his official bond, for all damages sustained, to be recovered by action of debt by said board, in their corporate name, for the use of the proper township, before any court having jurisdiction of the amount of damages claimed; but if such treasurer, in any such failure or refusal, acted under and in conformity to a requisition or order of said board, or a majority of them, entered upon their journal and subscribed by their president and clerk, then, and in that case, the members of the board aforesaid, or those of them voting for such requisition, or order aforesaid, and not the treasurer, shall be liable, jointly and severally, to the inhabitants of the township for such damages, to be recovered by an action of assumpsit in the official name of the county superintendent of schools, for the use of the proper townships: *Provided*, that said township treasurer shall be liable for any part of the judgment obtained against said trustees which cannot be collected on account of the insolvency of such trustees.

§ 21. Whenever a township treasurer shall resign or be removed, and at the expiration of his term of office, he shall pay over to his successor in office all money on hand, and deliver over all books, notes, bonds, mortgages and all other securities for money, and all papers and documents of every description in which the corporation has any lawful interest whatever. And in case of the death of the township treasurer, his securities and legal representatives shall be bound to comply with the requisitions of this section, so far as the said securuties and legal representatives may have the power so to do. And for a failure to comply with the requisities of this section, the persons neglecting or refusing shall be liable to a penalty of not less than ten dollars ($10) nor more than one hundred dollars ($100) at the discretion of the court before which judgment may be obtained, to be recovered in an action of debt, in the name of the trustees of schools, before any justice of the peace, for the benefit of the school fund of such township: *Provided* that the obtaining or payment of such judgment shall in no wise discharge or diminish the obligations of the persons signing the official bond of such township treasurer.

§ 22. The township treasurers shall receive in full, for all services rendered by them, a compensation to be fixed, prior to their election, by the board of trustees.

## ARTICLE V.

### BOARD OF DIRECTORS.

§ 1. Board of directors in districts with less than 1,000 inhabitants.
§ 2. Board of directors a body politic.
§ 3. Eligibility of school directors.
§ 4. Non-residence creates a vacancy.
§ 5. Annual election and term of office.
§ 6. Election in new districts.
§ 7. Vacancies.
§ 8. Notices of election.
§ 9. Election in certain cases ordered by township treasurer or county superintendent.
§ 10. Judges; postponement; election on any Saturday.
§ 11. A tie vote.
§ 12. Delivery of the poll-book, and filing the same; certificate.
§ 13. Poll-book in union district.
§ 14. Penalty for failure to deliver the poll-book
§ 15. Organization of the board.
§ 16. Quorum.
§ 17. Records.
§ 18. Meetings.
§ 18 Business to be done at a regular or special meeting.
§ 20. President or clerk pro tempore.
§ 21. Report of the organization.
§ 22. Reports of statistics, etc.
§ 23. Not to be interested in school contracts.
§ 24 Not to be interested in sale of school books, etc.
§ 25. Liable to indictment and fine.
§ 26. Duties defined.
§ 27. Additional powers defined.
§ 28. Orders on demand.
§ 29. Orders in anticipation of taxes.
§ 30. Liable for balance due teachers.
§ 31. Vote of the district required to locate school sites, etc.
§ 32. Compensation for school site.
§ 33. Removal by the county superintendent.
§ 34. Funds paid out upon orders; form of order.
§ 35. Transfer of pupils: separate schedules.
§ 36. Directors collect amount due from transfer pupils.

SECTION 1. In all school districts having a population of less than one thousand inhabitants, and not governed by any special act in relation to free schools now in force, there shall be elected in the manner hereinafter provided for, a board of directors to consist of three members. [As amended by an act approved June 1, 1889.

§ 2. The directors of each district are hereby declared a body politic and corporate, by the name of "school directors of District No. ...., township No. ....., range No. ....., county of ............, and State of Illinois," and by that name may sue and be sued in all courts and places whatever.

§ 3. Any person, male or female, married or single, of the age of twenty-one years and upwards, who is a resident of the school district, and who is able to read and write in the English language, shall be eligible to the office of school director: *Provided*, that no person shall be eligible to the office of school director who is at the time a member of the board of school trustees.

§ 4. If any director shall, during the term of his office, remove from the district in which he was elected, his office shall thereby become vacant and a new director shall be elected, as in other cases of vacancy in office.

§ 5. The annual election of school directors shall be on the third Saturday of April, when one director shall be elected in each district, who shall hold his office for three years, and until his successor is elected.

§ 6. In new districts, the first election of directors may be on any Saturday, notice being given by the township treasurer, as for the election of trustees, when three directors shall be elected, who shall, at their first meeting, draw lots for their respective terms of office, for one, two and three years.

§ 7. When vacancies occur, the remaining director or directors shall, without delay, order an election to fill such vacancies, which election shall be held on Saturday.

§ 8. Notices of all elections in organized districts shall be given by the directors at least ten days previous to the day of said election. Said notices shall be posted in at least three of the most public places in the district, and shall specify the place where such election is to be held, the time of opening and closing of the polls, and the question or questions to be voted on.

§ 9. Should the directors fail or refuse to order any regular or special election, as aforesaid, it shall be the duty of the township treasurer to order such election, and if the township treasurer fails to do so, then it shall be.the duty of the county superintendent to order such election of directors within ten days, in each case of such failure or refusal, and the election held in pursuance of such order shall be valid, the same as if ordered by the directors.

§ 10. Two of the directors ordering such election shall act as judges, and one as clerk of such election. But if said directors or any of them shall fail to order an election, to attend, or shall refuse to act when present, and in all unorganized districts and in elections to fill vacancies, the legal voters when assembled shall choose such additional members as may be necessary to act as two judges and a clerk of said election: *Provided,* that if upon the day appointed for said election, the said directors or judges shall be of opinion that, on account of the small attendance of voters the public good requires it, or if the voters present, or a majority of them, shall desire it, they shall postpone said election until the next Saturday, at the same place and hour, when the voters shall proceed as if it were not an adjourned meeting: *And, provided, also,* that if notice shall not have been given as above required, then said election shall be ordered as aforesaid and holden on any Saturday, notice thereof being given, as aforesaid.

§ 11. In case of a tie vote, the judges shall decide it by lot on the day of the election.

§ 12. Within ten days after every election of directors, the judges shall cause the poll-book to be delivered to the township treasurer, with a certificate thereon showing the election of said directors and the names of the persons elected; which poll-book shall be filed by the township treasurer, and shall be evidence of said election.

§ 13. In cases of a union district, made up of parts of two or more townships, the poll-book shall be returned to the township treasurer who receives the tax money for said district.

§ 14. For a failure to deliver the poll-book within the time prescribed, the judges shall be liable to a penalty of not less than twenty-five dollars ($25) nor more than one hundred dollars ($100) to be recovered in the name of the People of the State of Illinois, by action of assumpsit, before any justice of the peace of the county, which penalty, when recovered, shall be added to the township school fund of the township.

§ 15. The directors, within ten days after the annual election of the directors, shall meet and organize by appointing one of their number president, and another of their number clerk of such board of directors.

§ 16. Two directors shall be a quorum for business.

§ 17. The clerk of such board of directors shall keep a record of all the official acts of the board in a well-bound book provided for that purpose, which record shall be signed by the president and clerk, and shall be submitted to the township treasurer for his inspection and approval on the first Mondays of April and October, and at such other times as the township treasurer may require.

§ 18. The board of directors shall hold regular meetings at such times as they may designate; and they may hold special meetings as occasion may require, at the call of the president or any two members.

§ 19. No official business shall be transacted by the board except at a regular or special meeting.

§ 20. If the president or clerk be absent from any meeting, or, being present, refuses to perform his official duties, a president or clerk *pro tempore* shall be appointed.

§ 21. The clerk of each board of school directors shall report to the township treasurer or treasurers of the proper township or townships, immediately after the organization of the board, the names of the president and clerk of such board.

§ 22. On or before the seventh day of July, annually, the clerk of each board of directors shall report to the township treasurer having the custody of the funds of such district, such statistics and other information in relation to the schools of his respective district as the township treasurer is required to embody in his report to the county superintendent, and the particular statistics to be so reported shall be determined and designated by the State Superintendent of Public Instruction, or by the county superintendent.

§ 23. No director shall be interested in any contract made by the board of which he is a member.

§ 24. No director shall be interested in the sale, proceeds or profits of any book, apparatus or furniture used or to be used in any school in this State with which he may be connected.

§ 25. Any person offending against the provisions of the two preceding sections shall be liable to indictment, and, upon conviction, shall be fined in any sum not less than twenty-five dollars ($25) and not more than five hundred dollars ($500), and may be imprisoned in the county jail not less than one nor more than twelve months, at the discretion of the court.

§ 26. It shall be the duty of the board of directors of each district—

*First*—At the annual election of directors to make a detailed report of their receipts and expenditures to the voters there present, and transmit a copy of such report to the township treasurer within five days from the time of said election.

*Second*—To report to the county superintendent, within ten days after their employment, the full names of all persons employed as teachers, the date of the beginning and the end of their contract.

*Third*—To provide for the necessary revenue to maintain free schools in their district in the manner provided for in article VIII of this act.

*Fourth*—When a district is composed of parts of two or more townships, the directors shall determine and inform the collectors of said townships, and the collector or collectors of the county or counties in which said townships lie, in writing, under their hands as directors, which of the treasurers of the townships from which their district is formed shall demand and receive the tax money collected by the said collector as aforesaid.

*Fifth*—To establish and keep in operation for at least one hundred and ten (110) days of actual teaching, in each year, without reduction by reason of closing schools on legal holidays, or for any other cause, and longer if practicable, a sufficient number of free schools for the accommodation of all children in the district over the age of six (6) and under twenty-one (21) years, and shall secure for all such children the right and opportunity to an equal education in such free schools.

*Sixth*—To adopt and enforce all necessary rules and regulations for the management and government of the schools.

*Seventh*—To visit and inspect the schools from time to time as the good of the schools may require.

*Eighth*—To appoint all teachers and fix the amount of their salaries.

*Ninth*—The directors shall direct what branches of study shall be taught, and what text books and apparatus shall be used in the several schools, and strictly enforce uniformity of text books therein, but shall not permit text books to be changed oftener than once in four years, but shall prohibit such change.*

*Tenth*—The directors shall have power to purchase, at the expense of the district, a sufficient number of the text books used to supply children whose parents are not able to buy them. The text books bought for such purpose shall be loaned only, and the directors shall require the teacher to see that they are properly cared for and returned at the end of each term of school.

*Eleventh*—The directors shall, on or before the seventh day of July, annually, deliver to the township treasurer, all teachers' schedules made and certified as required by the provisions of article VII of this act, covering all time taught during the school year, ending June 30th, and the directors shall be personally liable to the district for any loss sustained by it, through the failure of the directors to examine and so deliver such schedules within the time fixed by law.

*Twelfth*—The directors shall not pay out any public money to any teacher unless such teacher shall, at the time of his or her employment, hold a certificate of qualification, obtained under the provisions of this act, covering the entire period of his or her employment.

*Thirteenth*—The directors shall not pay any public funds to any teacher unless such teacher shall have kept and furnished schedules as required by this act, and shall have satisfactorily accounted for books, apparatus and other property of the district that he may have taken in charge.

*Fourteenth*—The directors shall pay teachers' wages monthly. Upon the receipt of schedules, properly certified, the directors shall at once make out and deliver to the teacher an order upon the township treasurer for the amount named in the schedule; which order shall state the rate at which the teacher is paid according to his contract, the limits of time for which the order pays, and that the directors have duly certified a schedule covering this time. But it shall not be lawful for the directors to draw an order until they have duly certified to the schedule; nor shall it be lawful for the directors, after the date of filing schedules as fixed by law, to certify any schedule not delivered to them before that date by the teacher, when such schedule is for time taught before the first of July preceding, nor to give an order in payment of the teacher's wages for the time covered by such delinquent schedule.

*Fifteenth*—At the annual election of directors, the directors shall cause a copy of the township treasurer's report of the

---

* See act concerning alcohol and narcotics, approved June 1, 1889.

financial condition of the district, provided by law, to be posted
upon the front door of the building where such annual election
is held.

§ 27. The board of school directors shall be clothed with the
following additional powers:

*First*—To use any funds belonging to their district, and not
otherwise appropriated, for the purchase of a suitable book for
their records. And the said records shall be kept in a punctual,
orderly and reliable manner.

*Second*—Said directors may, where they deem the amount of
labor done sufficient to justify it, allow the clerk of such board
of directors, out of any fund not otherwise appropriated, compensation for duties actually performed.

*Third*—They shall have the power to dismiss a teacher for incompetency, cruelty, negligence, immorality or other sufficient cause.

*Fourth*—They shall have power to assign pupils to the several
schools in the district; to admit non-residents when it can be
done without prejudice to the rights of resident pupils; to fix
rates of tuition; collect and pay the same to the township treasurer for the use of said district.

*Fifth*—They may suspend or expel pupils who may be guilty
of gross disobedience or misconduct, and no action shall lie
against them for sucn expulsion or suspension.

*Sixth*—They may provide that children under twelve (12)
years of age shall not be confined in school more than four
hours daily.

*Seventh*—They may appropriate, for the purchase of libraries
and apparatus, any school funds remaining after all necessary
school expenses are paid.

*Eighth* —When any school district owns any personal property
not needed for school purposes, the directors of such district
may sell sucn property at public or private sale, as in their
judgment will be for the best interest of the district, and the proceeds of such sale shall be paid over to the treasurer of such
district, for the benefit of said school district.

*Ninth*—They may grant special holidays whenever in their
judgment such action is advisable: *Provided,* no teacher shall
be required to make up the time lost by the granting of such
holidays.

*Tenth*—They shall have the control and supervision of all school
houses in their district, and may grant the temporary use of
school houses when not occupied by schools, for religious meetings and Sunday schools, for evening schools and literary
societies, and for such other meetings as the directors may deem
proper.

*Eleventh*—They shall have power to decide when the school
house site, or the school buildings have become unnecessary, or
unsuitable, or inconvenient for a school.

*Twelfth*—They may borrow money, and issue bonds therefor, for building school houses, purchasing sites, repairing and improving school houses, in the way and manner provided for by article IX of this act.

§ 28. The school directors shall draw no order or warrant payable on demand upon the township treasurer or against any fund in his hands, unless at the time of drawing such order or warrant there are sufficient funds in his hands to pay the amount of the same: *Provided*, this section shall not apply to orders issued to teachers for their wages.

§ 29. Whenever there is no money in the treasury of any school district to meet and defray the ordinary and necessary expenses thereof, it shall be lawful for the board of directors to provide that all orders or warrants may be drawn and issued against and in anticipation of the collection of any taxes already levied by said directors for the payment of the ordinary and necessary expenses of any such district, to the extent of seventy-five per centum of the total amount of said tax levy: *Provided*, that warrants drawn and issued under the provisions of this section shall show upon their face that they are payable solely from said taxes when collected, and not otherwise, and such warrants shall be received by any collector of taxes in payment of the taxes against which they are issued, and which taxes against which said warrants or orders are drawn shall be set apart and held for their payment.

§ 30. The school directors shall be liable as directors for the balance due teachers, and for all debts legally contracted.

§ 31. It shall not be lawful for a board of directors to purchase or locate a school-house site, or to purchase, build or move a school house, or to levy a tax to extend schools beyond nine months without a vote of the people at an election called and conducted as required by section 4 of article IX of this act. A majority of the votes cast shall be necessary to authorize the directors to act: *Provided*, that if no one locality shall receive a majority of all the votes cast at such election, the directors may, if in their judgement the public interest re-site; so chosen by them shall, in such case, be legal and valid, the same as if it had been determined by a majority of the votes cast; and the site so selected by either of the methods above provided shall be the school-house site for such district; and said district shall have the right to take the same for the purpose of a school-house site either with or without the owner's consent, by condemnation or otherwise.

§ 32. In case the compensation to be paid for the school-house site mentioned in the preceding section cannot for any reason be agreed upon or determined between the school directors and the parties interested in the land taken for such site, then it shall be the duty of the directors of such district to proceed to have such compensation determined in the manner which may be at the time provided by law for the exercise of the right of eminent domain: *Provided*, that no tract of land lying outside of the limits of any incorporated city or village, and lying within forty rods of the dwelling house of the owner of the land, shall be taken for a school site without the owner's consent.

§ 33. Any director willfully failing to perform his duties as director under this act, may be removed by the county superintendent, and a new election ordered, as in other cases of vacancies.

§ 34. All funds belonging to any school district, and coming from any source, shall be paid out only on order of the board of directors, signed by the president and clerk of said board, or by a majority of said board. In all such orders shall be stated the purpose for which or on what account such order was drawn. Such order may be in the following form:

The treasurer of township No. ........., range No. ........., in.......... county, will pay to............ or bearer, ............ dollars and...... cents, (on his contract for repairing school house, or whatever the purpose may be). By order of the board of directors of school district No. ......, in said township.

> A...... B..........., *Presiden* 
> C...... D...........

§ 35. Pupils shall not be transferred * another without the written cor rectors of each district. w᠁ to and filed with ᠁ evidence ᠁

᠁es.
᠁ou is in the
᠁chool is taught, the
᠁er the separate schedules to
᠁who shall credit the district in which
᠁ught, and charge the other district with the
᠁amounts certified in said separate schedules to be due.
᠁pupils are transferred from a district of another township, the schedule for that district shall be delivered to the directors thereof, who shall immediately draw an order on their treasurer in favor of the treasurer of the township in which the school was taught for the amount certified to be due in said separate schedule.

§ 36. When a school is composed in part of pupils transferred, as provided for in the preceding section, from other townships, the duty of collecting the amount due on account of such pupils shall devolve upon the directors of the district in which the school was taught.

*Twelfth*—They may borrow money, and issue bonds therefor, for building school houses, purchasing sites, repairing and improving school houses, in the way and manner provided for by article IX of this act.

§ 28. The school directors shall draw no order or warrant payable on demand upon the township treasurer or against any fund in his hands, unless at the time of drawing such order or warrant there are sufficient funds in his hands to pay the amount of the same: *Provided,* this section shall not apply to orders issued to teachers for their wages.

§ 29. Whenever there is no money in the treasury of any school district to meet and defray the ordinary and necessary expenses thereof, it shall be lawful for the board of directors to provide that all orders or warrants may be drawn and issued against and in anticipation of the collection of any taxes already levied by said directors for the payment of the ordinary and necessary expenses of any such district, to the extent of seventy-five per centum of the total amount of said tax levy: *Provided,* that warrants drawn and issued under the provisions of this section shall show upon their face that they are payable solely from said taxes when collected, and not otherwise, and such warrants shall be received by any collector of taxes in payment of the taxes against which they are issued, and which taxes against which said warrants or orders are drawn shall be set apart and held for their payment.

§ 30. The school directors shall be liable as directors for the balance due teachers, and for all debts legally contracted.

§ 31. It shall not be lawful for a board of directors to purchase or locate a school-house site, or to purchase, build or move a school house, or to levy a tax to extend schools beyond nine months without a vote of the people at an election

### ERRATUM.

On page 46, Sec, 31, Art. V., insert the following line between lines nine and ten:

"quires it, proceed to select a suitable school house site; and the"

and said district shall have the right to take the same for the purpose of a school-house site either with or without the owner's consent, by condemnation or otherwise.

§ 32. In case the compensation to be paid for the school-house site mentioned in the preceding section cannot for any reason be agreed upon or determined between the school directors and the parties interested in the land taken for such site, then it shall be the duty of the directors of such district to proceed to have such compensation determined in the manner which may be at the time provided by law for the exercise of the right of eminent domain: *Provided*, that no tract of land lying outside of the limits of any incorporated city or village, and lying within forty rods of the dwelling house of the owner of the land, shall be taken for a school site without the owner's consent.

§ 33. Any director willfully failing to perform his duties as director under this act, may be removed by the county superintendent, and a new election ordered, as in other cases of vacancies.

§ 34. All funds belonging to any school district, and coming from any source, shall be paid out only on order of the board of directors, signed by the president and clerk of said board, or by a majority of said board. In all such orders shall be stated the purpose for which or on what account such order was drawn. Such order may be in the following form:

The treasurer of township No. ........, range No. ........, in.........
county, will pay to............ or bearer, ............ dollars and......
cents, (on his contract for repairing school house, or whatever the purpose may be). By order of the board of directors of school district No. ......, in said township.

A...... B..........., *President.*
C...... D..........., *Clerk.*

§ 35. Pupils shall not be transferred from one district to another without the written consent of a majority of the directors of each district, which written consent shall be delivered to and filed with the proper township treasurer, and shall be evidence of such consent. A separate schedule shall be kept for each district, and in each schedule shall be certified the proper amount due the teacher from that district, computed upon the basis of the total number of days' attendance of all schedules. If the district from which the pupils are transferred is in the same township as the district in which the school is taught, the directors of said district shall deliver the separate schedules to their township treasurer, who shall credit the district in which the school was taught, and charge the other district with the respective amounts certified in said separate schedules to be due. If pupils are transferred from a district of another township, the schedule for that district shall be delivered to the directors thereof, who shall immediately draw an order on their treasurer in favor of the treasurer of the township in which the school was taught for the amount certified to be due in said separate schedule.

§ 36. When a school is composed in part of pupils transferred, as provided for in the preceding section, from other townships, the duty of collecting the amount due on account of such pupils shall devolve upon the directors of the district in which the school was taught.

48

# ARTICLE VI.

### BOARD OF EDUCATION.

§ 1. Cities and villages.
§ 2. Boards of education in all districts not less than 1,000 inhabitants; number of members.
§ 3. President of the board.
§ 4. Duties and powers of the president.
§ 5. Annual election of members; term of office.
§ 6. Notice of election; form of notice.
§ 7. Election on any Saturday.
§ 8. Conduct of election.
§ 9. Election of members of board of education to succeed directors.
§ 10. Powers and duties of the board defined.
§ 11. Yeas and nays.
§ 12. Business to be done at a regular or special meeting.
§ 13. Conveyances of real estate; how made.
§ 14. School moneys in charge of township treasurer.
§ 15. Special acts may be relinquished; manner of change and form of notice.
§ 16. Redistricting under this act; election of school boards.

§ 17. Number of members in board of education of cities having over 100,000 inhabitants, and manner of their appointment.
§ 18. Eligibility to membership in boards of education in such cities.
§ 19. Organization; employés of the board; term, etc.
§ 20. Records; yeas and nays.
§ 21. Powers, with concurrence of city council defined.
§ 22. Other powers defined.
§ 23. Duties defined.
§ 24. Business to be done at a regular meeting.
§ 25. Conveyances of real estate made to city in trust.
§ 26. School moneys held by city treasurer.
§ 27. City not liable for excess of expenditures; board not authorized to tax.
§ 28. Powers of board not to be exercised by city council.

SECTION 1. Incorporated cities and villages, except such as now have charge and control of free schools by special acts, shall be and remain parts of the school townships in which they are respectively situated, and be subject to the general provisions of the school law, except as otherwise provided in this article.

§ 2. In all school districts having a population of not less than one thousand and not over one hundred thousand inhabitants, and not governed by any special act in relation to free schools now in force, there shall be elected, instead of the directors provided by law in other districts, a board of education, to consist of a president of the board of education, six members, and three additional members for every additional ten thousand inhabitants. Whenever additional members of such board of education are to be elected by reason of increased population of such district, such members shall be elected on the third Saturday of April succeeding the ascertaining of such increase by any general or special census, and the notice of such election shall designate the term for which the members are to be elected, so that one-third of the board shall be elected for each year: *Provided*, that in no case shall said board consist of more than fifteen members.

§ 3. The president of said board of education shall be elected annually, at the same time the members of the board of education are elected, and he shall hold his office for the term of one year, and until his successor is elected and qualified.

§ 4. The president of the board of education so elected shall preside at all meetings of said board, and shall give the casting vote in case of a tie between the members thereof; but otherwise he shall not have a vote. He shall sign all orders for the payment of money ordered by said board, and generally perform such duties as are imposed by law upon presidents of boards of directors, or that may be imposed upon him by said board of education, not in conflict with law: *Provided*, that in the absence or inability to act as said president, said board may appoint a president *pro tempore* from their number.

§ 5. The annual election of members of the board of education shall be on the third Saturday in April, when one-third of the members shall be elected for three years, and until their successors are elected and qualified.

§ 6. Notice of such election shall be given by the board of education at least ten days previous to such election by posting notices in at least three of the most public places in said district, which shall specify the place where such election is to be held, the time of opening and closing the polls and the purpose for which such election is held, which notice may be in the following form, to-wit:

Public notice is hereby given, that on Saturday, the ...... day of April A. D........, an election will be held at...................., between the hours of......, and ...... of said day, for the purpose of electing a president of the board of education of district No......, township No......, range No......, and ...... members of the board of education of said district.
Dated this........day of..............., A. D......
                                       A........ B........, *President.*
                                       C........ D........, *Clerk.*

§ 7. In case of a failure to give the notice above provided for, such election may be held on any Saturday after such notice has been give as aforesaid.

§ 8. Such election shall be conducted in the same manner, and be governed by the provisions of this act relating to the election of boards of directors, except as otherwise provided by law.

§ 9. At the first election of directors succeeding the passage of this act, in any district having a population of not less than one thousand (1,000) inhabitants by the census of 1880, and in such other districts as may hereafter be ascertained by any special or general census to have a population of not less than one thousand (1,000) inhabitants, at the first election of directors occurring after taking such special or general census, there shall be elected a board of education, who shall be the successors of the directors of the district; and all rights of property and all rights or causes of action existing or vested in such directors, shall vest in said board of education, in as full and complete a manner as was vested in the school directors. Such board, at its first meeting, shall fix, by lot, the terms of office of its members, so that one-third of them shall serve for one year, one-third for two years, and one-third for three years, and thereafter one-third shall be elected annually on the third Saturday in April, to fill the vacancies occurring, and to serve for the term of three years.

—4 S.

§ 10. The board of education shall have all the powers of school directors; and, in addition thereto and inclusive thereof, they shall have the power and it shall be their duty—

*First*—To establish and support free schools not less than six nor more than ten months in each year.

*Second*—To repair and improve school houses, and furnish them with the necessary fixtures, furniture, apparatus, libraries and fuel.

*Third*—To examine teachers as supplemental to any other examination, to employ teachers and to fix the amount of their salaries. [As amended by act approved June 19, 1893.

*Fourth*—To establish schools of different grades, and make regulations for the admission of pupils into the same.

*Fifth*—To buy or lease sites for school houses, with the necessary grounds: *Provided,* it shall not be lawful for such board of education to purchase or locate a school house site, or to purchase, build or move a school house, unless authorized by a majority of all voters voting at an election called for such purpose in pursuance of a petition signed by not less than five hundred (500) legal voters of such district, or by one-fifth of all the legal voters of such district.

*Sixth*—To levy a tax, annually, upon the taxable property of the district, in the manner provided in article VIII of this act, for the purpose of supporting and maintaining free schools in accordance with the powers herein conferred: *Provided,* that it shall not be lawful for such board of education to levy a tax to extend schools beyond a period of ten months in each year, except upon petition of a majority of the voters of the district: *And provided, further,* that all taxes shall be levied under the limitations relating to the percentage of the assessment, as provided by section 1, article VIII of this act.

*Seventh*—To employ, should they deem it expedient, a competent and discreet person or persons as superintendent or superintendents of schools, and fix and pay a proper salary or salaries therefor, and such superintendent may be required to act as principal or teacher in such schools.

*Eighth*—To lay off and divide the district into sub-districts, and from time to time alter the same, create new ones and consolidate them.

*Ninth*—To visit all the public schools as often as once a month to inquire into the progress of scholars and the government of the schools.

*Tenth*—To prescribe the method and course of discipline and instruction in the respective schools, and to see that they are maintained and pursued in the proper manner. *

*Eleventh*—To expel any pupil who may be guilty of gross disobedience or misconduct. No action shall lie against them for such expulsion.

---

* See act concerning alcohol and narcotics, approved June 1, 1889.

*Twelfth*—To dismiss and remove any teacher, whenever, in their opinion, he or she is not qualified to teach, or whenever, from any cause, the interests of the schools may, in their opinion, require such removal or dismissal.

*Thirteenth*—To apportion the scholars to the several schools.

*Fourteenth*—To establish and promulgate all such by-laws, rules and regulations for the government and the establishment and maintenance of a proper and uniform system of discipline in the several schools, as may, in their opinion, be necessary.

*Fifteenth*—To take charge of the school houses, furniture, grounds and other property belonging to the district, and see that the same are kept in good condition, and not suffered to be unnecessarily injured or deteriorated.

*Sixteenth*—To provide fuel and such other necessaries for the schools as, in their opinion, may be required in the school houses, or other property belonging to or under the control of the district.

*Seventeenth*—To appoint a secretary and provide well bound books at the expense of the school tax fund, in which shall be kept a faithful record of all their proceedings.

*Eighteenth*—To annually prepare and publish in some newspaper, or in pamphlet form, a report of the number of pupils instructed in the year preceding, the several branches of study pursued by them, of the number of persons between the ages of twelve and twenty-one unable to read and write, and the receipts and expenditures of each school, specifying the source of such receipts and the objects of such expenditures.

§ 11. In all questions involving the expenditure of money, the yeas and nays shall be taken and entered on the records of the proceedings of the board.

§ 12. None of the powers herein conferred upon boards of education shall be exercised by them, except at a regular or special meeting of the board.

§ 13. All conveyances of real estate shall be made to the township trustees in trust for the use of schools, and no conveyance of any real estate or interest therein used for school purposes, or held in trust for schools, shall be made, except by the board of trustees, upon the written request of such board of education.

§ 14. All money raised by taxation for school purposes, or received from the State common school fund, or from any other source, for school purposes, shall be held by the township treasurer as a special fund for school purposes, subject to the order of the board of education, upon warrants signed by the president and secretary thereof.

§ 15. Any city, incorporated town, township or district in which free schools are now managed under any special act, may, by vote of its electors, cease to control such schools under such special act, and become part of the school township in which it is situated, and subject to the control of the trustees thereof, under and according to the provisions of this act.

Upon petition of fifty voters of such city, town, township or district, presented to the board having control and management of schools in such city, town, township or district, it shall be the duty of such board, at the next ensuing election to be held in such city. town or township or district, to cause to be submitted to the voters thereof, giving not less than fifteen days' notice thereof, by posting not less than five notices in the most public places in such city, town, township or district, the question of "Organization under the Free School Law;" which notice may be in the following form, to-wit:

Public notice is hereby given that on the......day of.............A. D. ....an election will be held at ...................., between the hours of ......M. and......M. of said day, for the purpose of deciding the question of "Organization under the Free School Law."

§ 16. If it shall appear, on a convass of the returns of such election, that a majority of the votes cast at such election are "For Organization under the Free School Law," then at the next ensuing regular meeting of the board of trustees of the township or townships in which such city, incorporated town, town ship or district is situated, said trustees shall proceed to redistrict the township or townships as aforesaid, in such manner as shall suit the wishes and convenience of a majority of the inhabitants in their respective townships, and to make a division of funds and other property in the manner provided for by section 63 of article III of this act, and on any Saturday thereafter there shall be elected, in each of the new districts so formed, a director, directors or board of education, as the case may be, in the manner provided for in section 6 of article V of this act. and thereafter such districts shall proceed as other districts under this act; but all subsequent elections of directors or boards of education shall be conducted as provided in sections 5 and 8 of article V of this act. *

§ 17. In cities having a population exceeding one hundred thousand inhabitants, from and after this act shall take effect, the board of education shall consist of twenty-one members, to be appointed by the mayor, by and with the advice and consent of the common council, seven of whom shall be appointed for the term of one year, seven for the term of two years, and seven for the term of three years: *Provided, however*, that in such cities wherein there is now a board of education, holding their office by appointment, such officers shall continue in office until the time at which their terms would have expired under the law in force at the time of their appointment. At the expiration of the term of any members of said board, their successors shall be appointed in like manner and shall hold their office for the term of three years. Any vacancy which may occur shall be filled by the appointment of the mayor,

* See further provision in act approved June 2, 1891.

with the approval of the common council, for the unexpired term: *And, provided, further*, that from and after this act shall take effect there shall be appointed by the mayor, by and with the advice and consent of the common council, six members, two of whom shall be appointed for the term of one year, two for the term of two years, and two for the term of three years. [As amended by act approved June 22, 1891.

§ 18. Any person having resided in any such city more than five years next preceding his appointment, shall be eligible to membership of such board of education.

§ 19. The said board of education shall appoint a president and secretary, the president to be appointed from their own number, and shall appoint such other officers and employés as such board shall deem necessary, and shall prescribe their duties and compensation and terms of office.

§ 20. The said board shall provide well-bound books, at the expense of the school tax fund, in which shall be kept a faithful record of all their proceedings. The yeas and nays shall be taken and entered on the records of the proceedings of the board upon all questions involving the expenditure of money.

§ 21. The said board of education shall have charge and control of the public schools in such cities, and shall have power, with the concurrence of the city council—

*First*—To erect or purchase buildings suitable for school-houses, and keep the same in repair.

*Second*—To buy or lease sites for school-houses, with the necessary grounds.

*Third*—To issue bonds for the purpose of building, furnishing and repairing school houses, for purchasing sites for the same, and to provide for the payment of said bonds; to borrow money for school purposes upon the credit of the city.

§ 22. The said board of education shall have power—

*First*—To furnish schools with the necessary fixtures, furniture and apparatus.

*Second*—To maintain, support and establish schools, and supply the inadequacy of the school funds for the salaries of school teachers from school taxes.

*Third*—To hire buildings or rooms for the use of the board.

*Fourth*—To hire buildings or rooms for the use of schools.

*Fifth*—To employ teachers and fix the amount of their compensation.

*Sixth*—To prescribe the school books to be used, and the studies in the different schools.*

*Seventh*—To lay off and divide the city into school districts, and from time to time to alter the same and create new ones, as circumstances may require, and generally to have and pos-

*See act concerning alcohol and narcotics, approved June 1, 1889.

sess all the rights, powers and authority required for the proper management of schools, with power to enact such ordinances as may be deemed necessary and expedient for such purpose.

*Eighth*—To expel any pupil who may be guilty of gross disobedience or misconduct.

*Ninth*—To dismiss and remove any teacher whenever, in their opinion, he or she is not qualified to teach, or whenever, from any cause, the interests of the school may, in their opinion, require such removal or dismission.

*Tenth*—To apportion the scholars to the several schools.

*Eleventh*—To lease school property, and to loan moneys belonging to the school fund.

§ 23. It shall be the duty of such board of education—

*First*—To take the entire superintendence and control of the schools in such cities.

*Second*—To examine all persons offering themselves as candidates for teachers, and when found well qualified, to give them certificates gratuitously.

*Third*—To visit all the public schools as often as once a month.

*Fourth*—To establish all such by-laws, rules and regulations for the government and for the establishment and maintenance of a proper and uniform system of discipline in the several schools as may, in their opinion, be necessary.

*Fifth*—To determine from time to time, how many and what class of teachers may be employed in each of the public schools, and employ such teachers and fix their compensation.

*Sixth*—To take charge of the school-houses, furniture, grounds and other property belonging to the school districts, and see that the same are kept in good condition, and not suffered to be unnecessarily injured or deteriorated.

*Seventh*—To provide fuel and such other necessaries for the schools as, in their opinion, may be required in the school houses, or other property belonging to the said districts.

*Eighth*—To inquire into the progress of scholars and the government of the schools.

*Ninth*—To prescribe the method and course of discipline and instruction in the respective schools, and to see that they are maintained and pursued in the proper manner.

*Tenth*—To prescribe what studies shall be taught, and what books and apparatus shall be used.

*Eleventh*—To report to the city council, from time to time, any suggestions they may deem expedient or requisite in relation to the schools and the school fund, or the management thereof, and generally to recommend the establishment of new schools and districts.

*Twelfth*—To prepare and publish an annual report, which shall include the receipts and expenditures of each school, specifying the source of such receipts and the object of such expenditures.

*Thirteenth*—To communicate to the city council, from time to time, such information within their possession as may be required.

§ 24. None of the powers herein conferred upon the board of education of such cities shall be exercised by them except at a regular meeting of such board.

§ 25. All conveyances of real estate shall be made to the city in trust, for the use of schools, and no sale of real estate or interest therein, used for school purposes, or held in trust for schools, shall be made except by the city council, upon the written request of such board of education.

§ 26. All moneys raised by taxation for school purposes or received from the State common school fund, or from any other source for school purposes, shall be held by the city treasurer as a special fund for school purposes, subject to the order of the board of education, upon warrants to be countersigned by the mayor and city clerk.

§ 27. Said board of education shall not add to the expenditures for school purposes anything over and above the amount that shall be received from the State common school fund, the rental ·of school lands or property, and the amount annually appropriated for such purposes. If said board shall so add to such expenditure the city shall not, in any case, be liable therefor. And nothing herein contained shall be construed so as to authorize any such board of education to levy or collect any tax upon the demand, or under the direction of such board of education.

§ 28. All schools in such cities shall be governed as hereinbefore stated, and no power given to the board of education shall be exercised by the city council of such city.

## ARTICLE VII.

### TEACHERS.

§ 1. Age and qualifications; graduates of county normal schools,
§ 2. State certificates.
§ 3. First and second grade certificates; subjects for examination: renewal and revocation; form of certificate.
§ 4. Record by county superintendent.
§ 5. Must have a certificate.
§ 6. Subjects to be taught.
§ 7. Examinations by county superintendent.·
§ 8. Fee to be charged.
§ 9. Moneys thus received paid to county treasurer.
§ 10. Annual institute.
§ 11. No deduction of wages when attending institutes held on school days.
§ 12. Responsible for the property of the district.
§ 13. Must keep registers; form of register.
§ 14. Schedules, or statements of attendance to be made; form of schedule.
§ 15. Schedules to be delivered to directors; certificate of directors.
§ 16. Teacher's wages payable monthly; unpaid orders to draw interest.
§ 18. School month; holidays.

SECTION 1. No teacher shall be authorized to teach a common school under the provisions of this act who is not of good moral character, at least eighteen years of age, if a male, or seventeen years of age, if a female, and who does not possess a certificate of qualifications as hereinafter provided for: *Provided*, that in any county in which a county normal school is established, under the control of a county board of education, the diplomas of graduates in said normal school shall, when directed by said board, be taken by the county superintendent as sufficient evidence of qualification to entitle the holder to a first grade certificate; but such diplomas shall not be sufficient after two years from such graduation.

§ 2. The State Superintendent of Public Instruction is hereby authorized to grant State certificates to ' such teachers as may be found worthy to receive them; such certificates shall be of two grades, and both shall be valid in every county and school district in the State. The higher grade shall be valid during the lifetime of the holder, and the ·lower grade shall be valid for five years. But State certificates shall only be granted upon public examination, of which due notice shall be given, in such branches and upon such terms and by such examiners as the State Superintendent and the principals of the State universities may prescribe. Said certificates may be revoked by the State Superintendent upon proof of immoral or unprofessional conduct.* [As amended by an act approved April 28, 1893.

§ 3. It shall be the duty of the county superintendent to grant certificates to such persons as may, upon due examination, be found qualified. Said certificates shall be of two grades: those of the first grade shall be valid in the county for two years, and shall certify that the person to whom such certificate is given is of ♦ good moral character, and is qualified to teach orthography, reading in English, penmanship, arithmetic, English grammar, modern geography, the elements of the natural sciences, the history of the United States, physiology and the laws of health. Certificates of the second grade shall be valid for one year, and shall certify that the person to whom such certificate is given is of good moral character, and is qualified to teach orthography, reading in English, penmanship, arithmetic, English grammar, modern geography, and the history of the United States:* *Provided*, that teachers exclusively teaching music, drawing, penmanship, book-keeping, German or any other special study shall not be required to be examined except in reference to such special study; and, in such cases. it shall not be lawful to employ such teachers to teach any branch of study except such as they have been examined upon and which shall be stated in the certificate. The county superintendent may, in his option, renew said certificates at their expiration by his endorsement thereon, and may revoke the same at any time for immorality, incompetency, or other just cause. Said certificates may be in the following form, viz.:

---

* See act concerning alcohol and narcotics, approved June 1, 1889.

........................ Illinois, ...........A. D........
The undersigned, having examined..............in orthography, reading
in English, penmanship. arithmetic, English grammar, modern geography,
the history of the United States, and methods of teaching, and being
satisfied that......... ....is of good moral character, hereby certifies that
..............,.qualifications in the above branches are such as to entitle
..............to this certificate. being of the...........grade, and valid
in said county for..........year........from the date hereof, renewable at
the option of the county superintendent by his endorsement thereon.

Given under my hand and seal at the date aforesaid.

A. B.,
*County Superintendent of Schools.*

[As amended by an act approved June 21, 1895.]

§ 4. Each county superintendent shall also keep a record, in
a book provided for that purpose, of all teachers to whom he
grants certificates  Said record shall show the date and grade
of each certificate and all renewals granted, and the name, age
and nativity of each teacher; and shall give the names of male
and female teachers separately. Said record may be as follows,
viz.:

| Name. | Age. | Nativity. | Date. | Grade. | Experience. | Graduated. |
|---|---|---|---|---|---|---|
| Chas. Thompson. | 25 | Illinois. | March 1, 1888. | 1. | 5 years. | Has taught State Normal University |

§ 5. No teacher shall be entitled to any portion of the common school or township fund, or other public fund, or be employed to teach any school under the provisions of this act,
who shall not, at the time he enters upon his duties as such
teacher, have a certificate of qualification obtained under the
provisions of this act from the superintendent.of the State, or
the county superintendent of the county in which the school is
located, entitling him to teach. [As amended by act approved
June 19, 1893.]

§ 6. Every school established under the provisions of this
act shall be for instruction in the branches of education prescribed in the qualifications for teachers, and in such other
branches, including vocal music and drawing, as the directors,
or the voters of the district at the annual election of directors,
may prescribe.

§ 7. It shall be the duty of the county superintendents to
hold meetings, at least quarterly, and oftener if necessary, for
the examination of teachers, on such days and in such places
in the respective counties, as will, in their opinion, accommodate the greatest number of persons desiring such examination.
Notice of such meetings shall be published a sufficient length
of time, in at least one newspaper of general circulation, the
expense of such publication to be paid out of the school fund.

§ 8. The county superintendent shall in all cases require the
payment of a fee of one dollar from every applicant for examination for a teacher's certificate, and for each renewal of
such a certificate he shall require the payment of a fee of one
dollar.

§ 9. All moneys so received from applicants for teachers' certificates, and from the registration fees hereinafter provided for, the said county superintendent shall transmit monthly to the county treasurer, to be by him held and designated as the institute fund, and with such fund the county superintendent shall give the treasurer a list of the names of the persons paying such fees. Said fund shall be paid out by the county treasurer only upon the order of the county superintendent, and only to defray the expenses of the teachers' institutes, which the county superintendent is, by the following sections, authorized to hold. The county superintendent shall take vouchers for all payments made out of the institute fund, and he shall render an account of such disbursements, with vouchers for the same, to the county board at their regular meeting in September annually.

§ 10. The county superintendent shall hold, annually, a teachers' institute, continuing in session not less than five days, for the instruction of teachers and those who may desire to teach; and, with the concurrence of the State Superintendent of Public Instruction, procure such assistance as may be necessary to conduct said institute at such time as the schools of the county are generally closed: *Prov ded*, that two or more adjoining counties may hold an institute together. At every such institute, instruction shall be free to such as hold certificates good in the county (or counties where two or more join to hold an institute) in which the institute is held; but the county superintendent shall require all others attending to pay him a registration fee of one dollar, except those who have paid him an examination fee as required by section 8 of this article, and failed to receive a certificate.

§ 11. The time, not exceeding three days in any one term, or five days in any one school year, during term time, actually spent by a teacher of any public school in this State in attendance upon a teachers' institute, held under the direction of the county superintendent of schools, shall be considered time lawfully expended by such teacher in the service of the district where such teacher is employed, and no deduction of wages shall be made for such absences. And it shall be the duty of the school officers and boards of education to allow teachers to close their schools for such attendance upon such institute.

§ 12. It shall be the duty of every teacher employed in the public schools of the State to see that the school property of the district, placed under his care and control, is not unnecessarily damaged or destroyed. And no teacher shall be paid any part of the school funds, unless he shall have kept and furnished schedules (when required by law) as hereinafter directed, and shall also have satisfactorily accounted for all books, apparatus and other property belonging to the district, which he may have taken in charge.

§ 13. Teachers shall keep correct daily registers of their schools, which shall exhibit the name, age. and attendance of each pupil, the day of the week, the month and the year. Said registers shall be as nearly as may be, in the following form, the absence of each scholar being signified by a mark, the presence by a blank, viz:

Register of a common school kept by A. B., at...............in district No. ......, in township No. ........, range ...... of the ...... principal meridian, in the county of ............, in the State of Illinois.

| NAMES AND AGES OF SCHOLARS ATTENDING SCHOOL. | | 1888. Monday. January 15. | 1888. Tuesday. January 16. | 1888. Wednesday. January 17. | 1888. Thursday. January 18. | 1888. Friday. January 19. | 1888. Monday. January 23. | 1888. Tuesday. January 24. | 1888. Wednesday. January 25. | 1888. Th'urday. January 26. | 1888. Friday. January 29. | 1888. Monday. January 30. | 1888. Tuesday. January 31. | 1888. Wednesday. February 1. | 1888. Thursday. February 2. | 1888. Friday. February 3. | 1888. Monday. February 6. | 1888. Tuesday. February 7. | 1888. Wednesday. February 8. | 1888. Thursday. February 9. | 1888. Friday. February 9. | Total No. of days of each scholar |
|---|---|---|---|---|---|---|---|---|---|---|---|---|---|---|---|---|---|---|---|---|---|---|
| Names. | Ages. | | | | | | | | | | | | | | | | | | | | | |
| John Smith | 10 | .. | 1 | .. | .. | 1 | .. | .. | 1 | .. | 1 | .. | .. | 1 | .. | .. | .. | .. | .. | .. | 1 | 15 |
| Isaac Meisler | 13 | .. | .. | 1 | .. | .. | 1 | 1 | 1 | 1 | .. | .. | 1 | 1 | .. | .. | 1 | 1 | .. | .. | .. | 11 |
| Sarah Danforth | 16 | .. | .. | .. | .. | .. | .. | .. | .. | .. | .. | .. | .. | .. | .. | .. | .. | .. | .. | .. | .. | 20 |
| Mary Newman | 18 | .. | .. | .. | 1 | .. | .. | .. | .. | .. | .. | .. | .. | .. | .. | .. | .. | .. | .. | .. | 1 | 18 |
| Grand total No. of days | | .. | .. | .. | .. | .. | .. | .. | .. | .. | .. | .. | .. | .. | .. | .. | .. | .. | .. | .. | .. | 64 |

| | Males. | Females. | Total. |
|---|---|---|---|
| Number of Scholars | 2 | 2 | 4 |

Average daily attendance.............................................................3.2

Said register shall be furnished to the teachers by the school directors, and each teacher shall, at the end of his term of school, return his register to the clerk of the school board of the district. And no teacher shall be paid any part of the public funds unless he shall have accurately kept and returned the register as aforesaid.

§ 14. In all districts controlled by a board of directors, teachers shall make schedules of the names of all scholars under twenty-one (21) years of age attending school, in the form prescribed by this act, and when scholars reside in two (2) or more districts, townships or counties, separate schedules shall be kept for each district, township or county. Boards of education may require teachers under their control to make schedules as herein directed, or to make statements certifying the number of days' attendance for each month, as shown by their registers, which statements shall be certified to by the board of education, and be subject to the same requirements concerning payment of teacher's salary and filing as those made by this act concerning schedules. The schedules to be made and returned by the teacher shall be, as near as circumstances will permit, in the following form, viz.:

Schedule of common school kept by............... at ................, in district No. .........., township No. .........., range No. ........of the ........ principal meridian, in the county of ............. in the State of Illinois. Names and ages of scholars residing in district No. ........ in township No. ............. north, range ........ west, .......... county, who have attended in my school during the time beginning the ........ day of .... ...., 18.... and ending the ........ day of ........., 18...., during which time the school was in session ........ school days.

| Names. | Ages. | Days attended. |
|---|---|---|
| John Smith.................................................. .. ............... | 10 | 15 |
| Isaac Meisler................................................................. | 13 | 11 |
| Sarah Danforth................................................................ | 16 | 20 |
| Mary Newman................................................................. | 18 | 18 |
| Grand total number of days attendance................................... | ............. | 64 |

| | Males. | Females. | Total. |
|---|---|---|---|
| Number of scholars.............................................. | 2 | 2 | 4 |
| Average daily attendance...................................... | ............. | ............. | 3.2 |

And said teacher shall add up the whole number of days' attendance of each scholar, and make out the grand total number of days attendance. He shall also note the whole number of scholars, giving the males and females separately; the average daily attendance, and shall set the age of each pupil opposite the name of such pupil, as in the form above prescribed, and shall attach thereto his certificate, which shall be in the following form, viz.:

I certify that the foregoing schedule of scholars attending my school as therein named, and residing as specified in said schedule, to the best of my knowledge and belief, is correct.

A........ B........, *Teacher.*

§ 15. When the teacher shall have completed his or her schedule or schedules as provided in the foregoing section, he or she shall deliver it to some one of the directors, who shall, if requested, give the teacher a receipt for the same. And it shall be the duty of the said director, in connection with at least one other director of the board, to carefully examine such schedule or schedules, and after correcting all errors, if any, if they shall find such schedule to have been kept according to law, they shall certify to the same as near as practicable, in the following form, viz.:

STATE OF ILLINOIS, } ss.
................. County. }

We, the undersigned directors of district No. .........., township No. ........., range No. ........, in the county aforesaid, certify that we have carefully examined the foregoing schedule and find the same to be correct, and that the school was conducted according to law; that the teacher is paid as per contract ...... dollars per ........; that the sum of ...... dollars is now due ........ for services for the month ending .........;

that said teacher has a legal certificate of .........grade, and that the property of said district in charge of such teacher has been satisfactorily accounted for.

Witness our hands this...............day of. ............, A. D........

...........................
...........................
...........................

*Directors.*

§ 16. Teachers' wages are hereby declared due and payable monthly, and upon certifying to the schedule or statement, as hereinbefore provided for, the directors, or board of education, may at once make out and deliver to the teacher an order upon the township treasurer for the amount named in the schedule or statement; which order shall state the rate at which the teacher is paid according to his contract, the limits of the time for which the order pays, and that the directors have duly certified a schedule covering the time specified in such order: *Provided,* that in case said order shall be presented to the township treasurer and not paid for want of funds, said treasurer shall certify on the back of such order the date of presentation as required by section 18 of article IV of this act, and thereafter such order shall bear interest at the rate of eight per cent. per annum until paid, or until the said treasurer shall notify the clerk of the board of directors issuing such order that he has funds with which to pay the same.

§ 17. The school month shall be the same as the calendar month, but teachers shall not be required to teach upon Saturdays, Sundays, legal holidays, these being New Year's, Fourth of July, Christmas and Thanksgiving, and fast days appointed by the national or state authority; nor shall they be required to make up the time lost by closing school upon such days or upon such special holidays as may be granted the schools by the board of directors.

## ARTICLE VIII.

### REVENUE-TAXATION.

§ 1. Power to tax; limitations.
§ 2. Certificate of tax levy; time of return; form.
§ 3. Return of certificate to county clerk; map filed.
§ 4. District in two counties.
§ 5. Taxes computed by county clerk.
§ 6. Assessors to designate the district.
§ 7. County clerk to copy numbers of districts; tax to be uniform.
§ 8. Certificate of amount due each district.
§ 9. Collector to pay township treasurer.
§ 10. Districts lying in two townships.
§ 11. Penalty for failure to pay.
§ 12. Blank books and notices.
§ 13. Failure to file certificate does not vitiate the assessment.

SECTION 1. For the purpose of establishing and supporting free schools, for not less than five nor more than nine months in each year, and defraying all the expenses of the same of every description; for the purpose of repairing and improving school houses, of procuring furniture, fuel, libraries and apparatus, and for all other necessary incidental expenses in each district, village or city, anything in any special charter to the contrary notwithstanding, the directors of such district, and the authorities of such village or city shall be authorized to levy a tax annually upon all the taxable property of the district. village or city, not to exceed two per cent. for educational, and three per cent. for building purposes (except to pay indebtedness contracted previous to the passage of this act,) the valuation to be ascertained by the last assessment for State and county taxes.

§ 2. The directors of each district shall ascertain, as near as practicable, annually, how much money must be raised by special tax for school purposes during the ensuing year, which amount shall be certified and returned to the township treasurer on or before the first Tuesday in August, annually. The certificate of the directors may be in the following form, viz.:

We hereby certify that we require the sum of.............dollars. to be levied as a special tax for school purposes, and..........dollars for building purposes, on the taxable property of our district, for the year A.. D........
Given under our hands this........day of........A. D......

A. B., ⎫ Directors district No........., township
C. D., ⎬ No........., range No........., county
E. F., ⎭ of........., State of Illinois.

§ 3. It shall be the duty of township treasurer to return the certificate mentioned in the foregoing section to the county clerk, on or before the second Monday of August, and whenever the boundaries of the districts of the townships shall have been changed, the township treasurer shall return to the county clerk, with the certificates, a map of the township, showing such changes, and certified as required by the provisions of this act.

§ 4. When a district lies partly in two or more counties. the directors thereof shall ascertain as nearly as practicable the amount to be raised by special tax for school purposes, and shall prepare one certificate thereof for each county in which such district may lie, and deliver all of the said certificates to the township treasurer, who receives the tax money of such district, who shall return one each of such certificates to the county clerk of each county within which such district shall lie. On the first Monday of October, or as soon thereafter as may be practicable, annually, the county clerk of each of such counties shall ascertain the total equalized valuation of all the taxable property in that part of such district as shall lie in his county, and certify the amount thereof to the county clerk of each of the other counties in which such district may lie; and from the aggregate of such equalized valuation and from the certificate of the amount so required to be levied, such clerks shall ascertain the rate per cent. required to produce in such district the amount of such levy, and at that rate shall extend the special tax to be levied for school purposes in that part of such district lying in their respective counties. [As amended by act approved June 17, 1891.

§ 5. According to the amount certified, as aforesaid, the county clerk, when making out the tax books for the collector, shall compute each taxable person's tax, in said district, upon the total amount of taxable property, as equalized by the State Board of Equalization for that year, lying and being in said district, whether belonging to residents or non-residents, and also each and every tract of land assessed by the assessor, which lies, or the largest part of which lies, in said district The said county clerk shall cause each person's tax, so computed, to be set upon the tax book to be delivered to the collector for that year, in a separate column, against each taxpayer's name or parcel of taxable property, as it appears in said collector's books, to be collected in the same manner and at the same time and by the same persons as State and county taxes are collected.

§ 6. It shall be the duty of assessors, when making assessments of personal property, to designate the number of the school district in which each person so assessed resides; which designation shall be made by writing the number of such district opposite each person's assessment of personal property, in a column provided for that purpose, in the assessment roll returned by the assessor to the county clerk.

§ 7. It shall be the duty of the county clerk to copy said numbers of school districts, so returned by the assessor, into the collector's book and to extend the school tax on each person's assessment of personal property, according to the rate required by the amount designated by the directors of the school district in which such person resides. The computations of each person's tax and the levy made by the clerk, as aforesaid, shall be final and conclusive: *Provided*, the rate shall be uniform and shall not exceed that required by the amount certified by the board of directors.

§ 8. The county clerk before delivering the tax book to the collector, shall make out and send by mail, to each township treasurer in the county, a certificate of the amount due each district or fraction of a district in his township, of said tax so levied and placed upon the tax books.

§ 9. On or before the first day of April next, after the delivery of the tax books containing the computation and levy of the said taxes, or so soon thereafter as the township treasurer shall present the said certificate of the amount of the said tax, and make a demand therefor, the said collector shall pay to said township treasurer the full amount of said tax so certified by the county clerk, or in case any part thereof remains uncollected, said collector shall, in addition to the amount collected, deliver to said township treasurer a statement of the uncollected taxes for each district of such township, taking of the township treasurer his receipt therefor, which receipt shall be evidence as well in favor of the collector as against the township treasurer. The said treasurer shall enter the amount collected in his books under the proper heads, and pay the same out as provided for by this act.

§ 10. When a district is composed of parts of two or more townships, the directors shall determine and inform the collectors of said townships, and the collector or collectors of the county or counties in which said townships lie, in writing, under their hands as directors, which of the treasurers of the townships, from which their district is formed, shall demand and receive the tax money collected by the said collectors as aforesaid.

§ 11. If any collector shall fail to pay the amount of said tax, or any part thereof, as required by the provisions of section nine (9) of this article, of this act, it shall be competent for the township treasurer, or other authorized person, to proceed against said collector and his securities in any action of debt upon his official bond, in any court of competent jurisdiction. And the said collector so in default shall pay twelve per centum upon the amount due, to be assessed as damages, which shall be included in the judgment rendered against him: *Provided*, no collector shall be liable for such part of said tax as he shall be able to make appear he could not have collected by law, until he has collected or may be able to so collect such amount.

§ 12. It is hereby made the duty of the proper officers in preparing blank books and notices for the use of assessors to provide columns and blanks for the use of assessors, so that they may designate the number of the school district, as provided for in section six (6) of this article of this act.

§ 13. A failure by the directors to file their certificates, or of the township treasurer to return the same to the county clerk in the time required by this act, shall not vitiate the assessment, but the same shall be as legal and valid as if completed in the time required by law.

## ARTICLE IX.

### BONDS.

§ 1. Vote necessary to borrow money; limit of sum borrowed.
§ 2. Registry of bonds
§ 3. Money paid into school treasury of township; cancellation of bonds.
§ 4. Election for borrowing money; form of notice.
§ 5. Judges.
§ 6. Poll book returned; penalty for failure to return poll book.
§ 7. Refunding school district bonds.

SECTION 1. For the purpose of building school houses or purchasing school sites, or for repairing and improving the same, the directors of any school district, when authorized by a majority of all the votes cast at an election called for that purpose, may borrow money, issuing bonds signed by not less than two members of said board of directors, in sums of not less than one hundred dollars ($100), and ˙bearing interest at a rate not exceeding eight per centum per annum: * *Provided*, that the sum borrowed in any one year shall not exceed five per cent. (including existing indebtedness) of the taxable property of the district, to be ascertained by the last assessment for State and county taxes previous to the incurring of such indebtedness.

§ 2. All bonds authorized to be issued by virtue of the foregoing section before being so issued, negotiated and sold, shall be registered, numbered and countersigned by the school treasurer of the township wherein the school house of such district is, or is to be located. Such register shall be made in a "bond register" book to be kept for that purpose, and in this register shall first be entered the record of the election authorizing the directors to borrow money, and then a description of the bonds issued by virtue of such authority as to number, date, to whom issued, amount, rate of interest and when due.

§ 3. All moneys borrowed under the authority granted by this article of this act, shall be paid into the school treasury of the township wherein the bonds issued therefor are required to be registered, and, upon receiving such moneys, the treasurer shall deliver the bond or bonds issued therefor to the parties entitled to receive the same, and shall credit the funds received to the district issuing the bonds. The treasurer of said township shall enter in the said "bond register" the exact amount received for each and every bond issued. And when any such bonds are paid, the said township treasurer shall cancel the same and shall enter in the said "bond register," against the record of such bonds, the words, "paid and cancelled the ......day of........, A. D., ........," filling the blanks with the day month and year corresponding with the date of such payment.

§ 4. Whenever it is desired to hold an election for the purpose of borrowing money, as provided for in this article of this act, the directors of the district in which such election is to be held, shall give at least ten days' notice of the holding of such election, by posting notices in at least three of the most public places in such district. Such notices shall specify the place where such election is to be held, the time of opening and closing the polls, and the question or proposition to be voted upon, which notice may be substantially in the following form, viz.:

NOTICE OF ELECTION.

Public notice is hereby given that on the........ day of .............. A. D......, an election will be held at .................. school district No......, in township No......, range No......, of the principal meridian

---

* 7 per cent. is the highest rate allowed by law on loans made on or after July 1, 1891.

—5 S

in....................county, Illinois, for the purpose of voting "For" or "Against" the proposition to issue the bonds of said school district No.. to the amount of......................dollars due (here insert the times of payment, giving the amount falling due each year, if the bonds mature at different dates), which bonds are to bear interest at the rate of...... per cent. per annum, payable........annually.

The polls of said election will be opened at......o clock....M., and will remain open until......o'clock....M.

Dated this................day of................ ...., A. D......

A. B.,<br>
C. D.,<br>
E. F.,<br>
Directors.

§ 5. At such election two of the directors of such district shall act as judges and one of said directors shall act as clerk. In case either or any of said directors shall fail, from any cause, to be present or to act at such election, at the time of opening the polls thereof, the legal voters assembled shall choose, from their number, persons to act as such two judges, and a clerk of said election. The said judges and the said clerk shall take and subscribe the oath required of judges and clerks of an election held for State or county officers, and such oath may be administered in the same manner as is or may be provided by law for administering the oath to judges and clerks at a State or county election. At such election all votes shall be by ballot. In districts which have adopted the provisions of, "An act regulating the holding of elections, and declaring the result thereof in cities, villages and incorporated towns in this State," approved June 19, 1885, the said election shall be held under the provisions of said act.

§ 6. Within ten days after every such election, the judges shall cause the poll-book to be returned to the township treasurer, who is required to register such bonds, with a certificate thereon showing the result of such election, which poll-book shall be filed and safely kept by the said township treasurer, and shall be evidence of such election. For a failure to return such poll-book to such treasurer within the time prescribed, the judges of said election shall severally be liable to a penalty of not less than twenty-five dollars ($25) nor more than one hundred dollars ($100), to be recovered in a suit in the name of the People of the State of Illinois, before any justice of the peace, and, when collected, shall be added to the township school fund of the township in which said treasurer resides.

§ 7. In all cases where any school district has heretofore issued or may hereafter issue bonds, or other evidences of indebtedness, for money on account of any public school building, or other public improvement, or for any other purposes which are now binding and subsisting legal obligations against said school district, and remaining outstanding, and which are properly authorized by law, the proper authorities of such school district may, upon the surrender of any such bonds or other evidences of indebtedness, or any number thereof, issue in place or in lieu thereof, or to take up the same, to the holders or owners of the same, or to other persons for money with which to take up the same, new bonds or other evidences of indebtedness, in such form, for such amount, upon such time, not exceeding the term of twenty (20) years, and drawing such rate of interest not ex- ceeding eight (8) per centum per annum,* as may be determined upon; and such new bonds or other evidences of indebtedness so issued shall show, on their face, that they are issued under this act: *Provided,* that the issue of such new bonds in lieu of such indebtedness shall first be authorized by a vote of the legal voters of such school district voting at an election called and conducted as other elections provided for by this article of this act: *And, provided, further,* that such bonds or other evidences of indebtedness shall not be issued so as to increase the aggregate indebtedness of such school district beyond five (5) per centum on the value of the taxable property therein, to be ascertained by the last assessment for State and county taxes, prior to the issuing of such bonds or other evidences of indebtedness.

## ARTICLE X.

### COUNTY CLERK.

§ 1. To furnish to county superintendent a list of trustees elected.
§ 2. To file papers relating to changes in district boundaries; penalty for failure to do so.
§ 3. To furnish certificate of equalized value of taxable property in case of district in two counties.
§ 4. To furnish certificate of equalized value of taxable property to any district.
§ 5. To compute tax; to copy the numbers of districts; to extend tax and to send certificate of amount due each district, etc.
§ 6. To certify to bills of county superintendents, and transmit them to State Auditor.
§ 7. To record land sales reported by county superintendent.

SECTION 1. In all cases where, by any provision of laws, the returns of any election for school trustees are made to the county clerk of any county, it shall be the duty of the county clerk, within ten days after such returns have been made to him, as aforesaid, to furnish to the county superintendent of schools a list of all such trustees so returned to him, and the township from which the same have been so returned.

§ 2. Whenever any change shall be made in the boundaries of any school district, and a written statement or record of such change shall be delivered to the county clerk of such county, it shall be the duty of said county clerk to file such statement or record, and all papers relating thereto, and duly record the same in the records of his office; and in case of neglect or failure so to do, the said county clerk shall be liable to a penalty of twenty-five dollars ($25), to be recovered by an action of debt before any justice of the peace, at the suit of the county superintendent, for the benefit of the school fund of the said county.

* 7 per cent. is the highest rate allowed by law, on loans made on or after July 1, 1891.

§ 3. Whenever any school district lies partly in two or more counties, it shall be the duty of the county clerk of each county in which any part of such district lies to furnish, upon request, to the directors of such district a certificate showing the last ascertained equalized value of the taxable property in that part of such district lying in such county.

§ 4. It shall be the duty of the county clerk to furnish to the directors of any school district, or to the board of education in districts having a board of education, upon request, a certificate showing the last ascertained equalized value of the taxable property of such district, as the same appears of record in his office.

§ 5. It shall be the duty of the county clerk, when making out the tax books for the collector, to compute each taxable person's tax in each school district, upon the total amount of taxable property, as equalized by the State Board of Equaliza- tion for that year, lying and being in such district, whether belonging to residents or non-residents, and also each and every tract of land assessed by the assessor which lies, or the largest part of which lies, in such district. Such computation shall be made so as to realize the amount of money required to be raised in such district, as shown and set forth in the certificate of tax levy, made out by the directors of such district, and filed with the township treasurer, as required by the provisions of this act. The said county clerk shall cause each person's tax, so computed, to be set upon the tax book to be delivered to the collector for that year, in a separate column against each tax payer's name, or parcel of taxable property, as it appears in said collector's books, to be collected in the same manner, and at the same time, and by the same person, as State and county taxes are collected. In making up the tax books to be delivered to the collectors of taxes, the county clerk shall copy into such tax books the number of the school district set opposite to each person's assessment of personal property by the assessor making the assessment of such person, and to ex- tend the school tax on each person's assessment of personal property, according to the rate required by the amount des- ignated by the directors of the school district in which such person resides, as shown by said certificate of tax levy. The computation of each person's tax and the levy made by the clerk, as aforesaid, shall be final and conclusive: *Provided*, that the rate shall be uniform, and shall not exceed that required by the amount certified by the board of directors. The said county clerk, before delivering the tax book to the collector, shall make out and send by mail to each township treasurer of the county a certificate of the amount due each district, or fraction of a district, in his township, of said tax so levied and placed upon the tax books. .

§ 6. Whenever the county board of any county shall have audited the itemized bills of the county superintendents of

schools or their assistants, as required by the provisions of
this act, it shall be the duty of the county clerk of such county
to certify to such act, and transmit the said bills to the Auditor
of Public Accounts, who shall, upon the receipt of them, remit,
in payment thereof to each superintendent, his warrant upon
the State Treasurer for the amount certified to be due him:
and the Auditor, in making his warrant to any county for the
amount due from the state school fund, shall deduct from it
the several amounts for which warrants have been issued to
the county superintendent of said county since the next preceding apportionment of the state school fund.

§ 7. The county clerk of each county shall preserve and
record in a well-bound book to be kept for that purpose, the
report of the county superintendent, made to the county board
at the first regular term of such board in each year, relating
to the sale of school lands, the amount of money received, paid,
loaned out and on hand, belonging to each township fund in
his control, and the statement copied from the loan book of
such county superintendent, showing all the facts in regard to
loans, which are required to be stated on the loan book.

## ARTICLE XI.

### COUNTY BOARD.

§ 1. Powers of the county board defined.
§ 2. Duties of the county board defined.
§ 3. Statement of land sales by the county board.

SECTION 1. The county board of each county of this State
shall have power—

*First*—To approve the bond of the county superintendent of
schools.

*Second*—To increase the penalty of the bond of the county
superintendent of schools beyond twelve thousand dollars
($12,000) if, in the discretion of said county board, such bond
should be so increased.

*Third*—To remove the county superintendent of schools from
office for any palpable violation of law or omission of duty.*

*Fourth*—To require the county superintendent of schools,
after notice given, to execute a new bond, conditioned and approved as the first bond, whenever in the discretion of the
county board such new bond is necessary: *Provided, however*,
that the execution of such new bond shall not affect the old
bond or the liability of the security thereof.

*Fifth*—To require the county superintendent of schools to
make the reports to such board provided for by law, and to
remove him from office in case of neglect or refusal so to do.

*Sixth*—In counties having not more than one hundred (100)
schools, the board may limit the time of the superintendent of
schools: *Provided*, that in the counties having not more than

* This grant of power is not annulled by the repeal of section 7, article 11.

fifty (50) schools the limit of time shall not be less than one hundred and fifty (150) days a year; in counties having from fifty-one (51) to seventy-five (75) schools, not less than two hundred (200) days a year; and in counties having from seventy-six (76) to one hundred (100) schools, not less than two hundred and fifty (250) days.

*Seventh*—Said county board shall authorize the county superintendent of schools to employ such assistants as he needs for the full discharge of his duties, and said county board shall fix the compensation to be paid therefor, which compensation shall be paid out of the county treasury.

§ 2. It shall be the duty of the county board of each county of this State—

*First*—To provide for the county superintendent of schools a suitable office with necessary furniture and office supplies as is done in the case of other county officers.

*Second*—When the office of county superintendent of schools shall become vacant by death, resignation, removal or otherwise, to fill the same by appointment. And the person so appointed shall hold his office until the next election of county officers, at which election the said board shall order the election of a successor.

*Third*—To examine and approve or reject the report of the county superintendent of schools made to such board, and the notes and securities taken by such superintendent for school funds.

*Fourth*—At the regular meeting in September, and as near quarterly thereafter, as such board may have regular or special meetings, to audit the itemized bills of the county superintendent, and of his assistants, for their per diem compensation and expenses allowed by law for visiting schools.

§ 3. At the first regular term of the county board, in each year, the county superintendent shall present to the county board of his county—

*First*—A statement showing the sales of school lands made subsequent to the first regular term of the previous year, which shall be a true copy of the sale book (book B).

*Second*—Statements of the amount of money received, paid, loaned out and in hand, belonging to each township or fund under his control, the statement of each fund to be separate.

*Third*—Statements copied from his loan book (book C), showing all the facts in regard to loans which are required to be stated on the loan book.

All of which the county board shall thereupon examine and compare with the vouchers, and the said county board, or so many of them as may be present at the meeting of the board, shall be liable individually to the fund injured and to the securities of the county superintendent, in case judgment be recovered of the said securities, for all damages occasioned by a neglect of the duties or any of them, required of said board by this section: *Provided*, nothing herein contained shall be construed to exempt the securities of said county superintendent from any liability as such securities, but they shall still be liable to the fund injured the same as if the members of the county board were not liable to them for neglect of their duty.

## ARTICLE XII.

### SCHOOL FUNDS.

§ 1. To consist of a two-mill tax; interest of school fund proper and of surplus revenue.
§ 2. State to pay interest.
§ 3. Dividend to counties made by State Auditor.
§ 4. Warrants issued by the State Auditor, and received from the collectors by State Treasurers.
§ 5. County superintendent to proceed against collector on his refusal to pay.
§ 6. Proceeds of the sale of sixteenth section, etc., constitute principal of township fund, etc.; interest distributed.
§ 7. Moneys paid out upon orders.
§ 8. Form of orders; filing of orders.
§ 9. Union districts; receipts to be taken.
§ 10. Loans in districts under a special charter.

SECTION 1. The common school fund of this State shall consist of the proceeds of a two-mill tax to be levied upon each dollar's valuation of the property in the State, annually, until otherwise provided by law; the interest on what is known as the school fund proper; being three per cent. upon the proceeds of the sales of the public lands in the State, one-sixth part excepted, and the interest on what is known as the surplus revenue, distributed by act of congress and made a part of the common school fund by act of the legislature, March 4, 1837.

§ 2. The State shall pay the interest mentioned in the preceding section at the rate of six per cent. per annum, annually, to be paid into, and become a part of, said school fund.

§ 3. On the first Monday in January in each and every year next after taking the census of the State, by federal or state authority, the Auditor of Public Accounts shall ascertain the number of children in each county in the State, under twenty-one years of age, and shall thereupon make a dividend to each county of the sum from the tax levied and collected under the provisions of the first section of this article of this act, and of the interest due on the school fund proper and surplus revenue, in proportion to the number of children in each county under the age aforesaid, and issue his warrant to the superintendent of schools of each county upon the collector thereof. Upon presentation of said warrant by the county superintendent to the collector of his county, said collector or the treasurer shall pay over to the county superintendent the amount of said warrant out of the first funds which may be collected by him and not otherwise appropriated by law, taking said superintendent's receipt therefor.

§ 4. The said warrants issued by the Auditor of Public Accounts for the school fund tax, and for the interest of the school fund proper and surplus revenue, shall be received by the State Treasurer in payment of amounts due the State from county collectors; and on presentation by the State Treasurer of said warrants to said Auditor, he shall issue his warrant to said Treasurer of the school fund, for the amount of the school fund tax warrants, and on the revenue fund for the amount of the warrants for interest on the school fund proper and surplus revenue. Dividends shall be made as aforesaid, according to the proportions ascertained to be due to each county annually, thereafter, until another census shall have been taken, and then dividends shall be made and continued as aforesaid, according to the last census.

§ 5. If any collector shall fail or refuse to pay the amount of the aforesaid Auditor's warrant, or any part thereof, by the first day of March annually, or as soon thereafter as it may be presented, it shall be competent for the county superintendent to proceed against said collector and his securities in an action of debt, in any court having competent jurisdiction, and the said collector shall pay interest at the rate of twelve per centum per annum, to be assessed as damages, upon the amount due, and which interest shall be included in the judgment obtained against him: *Provided*, that if it satisfactorily appears to the court that on said first day of March, or on the day of presentation for payment thereafter, that said collector had not, as yet, collected funds sufficient to pay said warrant, said interest shall not be allowed upon said warrant.

§ 6. All bonds, notes, mortgages, moneys and effects which have heretofore accrued or may hereafter accrue from the sale of the sixteenth section of the common school lands of any township or county, or from the sale of any real estate or other property taken on any judgment or for any debt due to the principal of any township or county fund, and all other funds of every description which have been or may hereafter be carried to and made part of the principal of any township or county fund, by any law which has heretofore been, is now or may hereafter be enacted, are hereby declared to be and shall forever constitute the principal of the township or county fund, respectively; and no part thereof shall ever be distributed or expended for any purpose whatever, but the same shall be loaned out and held to use, rent or profit, as provided by law. But the interest, rents, issues and profits, arising and accruing from the principal of said township or county fund, shall be distributed in the manner and at the times as provided by this act; nor shall any part of such interest, rents, issues and profits be carried to the principal of the respective funds, except it appear on the first Monday in October in any year, that there is rent, interest or other funds on hand which are not required for distribution, such amount not required, as aforesaid, may, if the board of trustees see proper, forever be considered as principal in the funds to which it belongs and loaned as such.

§ 7. School funds collected from special taxes, levied by order of school directors, or from the sale of property belonging to any district, shall be paid out only on the order of the proper board of directors; and all other moneys or school funds liable to distribution, paid into the township treasury, or coming into the hands of the township treasurer, shall, after said funds have been apportioned by the township trustees, as required in section 26 of article III of this act, be paid out only on the order of the proper board of directors, signed by the president and clerk of said board, or by a majority of said board. For all payments made, receipts shall be taken and filed by said board of directors.

§ 8. In all such orders shall be stated the purpose for which or on what account drawn. Said orders may be in the following form, viz.: .

The treasurer of township No......, range No......, in.........county, will pay to............or order, ......dollars and......,cents (on his contract for repairing school house, or whatever the case may be).

By order of the board of directors of school district No,.....; in said township.

A. B., *President.*
C. D., *Clerk.*

Which order, together with the receipt of the person to whom paid, shall be filed in the office of the township treasurer: *Provided,* that when an order is paid in full, such order, if properly endorsed by the person in whose favor it was drawn, and his assigns, if any, shall be a sufficient receipt for the purposes of this section.

§ 9. When a district is composed of parts of two or more townships, the township treasurer or treasurers who do not receive the tax money of said district, shall, when they hold any funds belonging to said district, notify the directors thereof of the amount of such funds, and the directors shall thereupon give the treasurer who receives the tax money of said district an order for such funds, and upon receipt thereof he shall hold them, to be paid out as aforesaid.

§ 10. In all cases where school funds are held by any person or persons in an official capacity, by virtue of any special charter defining the manner of loaning the same, such money may be loaned upon the same terms and conditions as are provided by this act, or may hereafter be provided, by the school laws of this State, for loaning the school funds of counties or townships.

74

## ARTICLE XIII.

### SCHOOL LANDS.

§ 1. Section sixteen
§ 2. Business relating to school lands, where transacted.
§ 3. Renting and sale of school lands.
§ 4. Right of way and depot grounds for use of railroads.
§ 5. Trespass on school land; penalty.
§ 6. Trespasser liable to indictment.
§ 7. Penalties and fines to be paid to township treasurer.
§ 8. Petition for sale.
§ 9. Fractional township.
§ 10. Divided into lots by trustees.
§ 11. Making of a plat.
§ 12. Size of lots, roads and streets.
§ 13. Valuation plats and certificate given to county superintendent.
§ 14. Advertising the sale; form of notice.

§ 15. Place of sale.
§ 16. Terms of sale; amount of bid borrowed.
§ 17. Manner of sale.
§ 18. Payment; land resold; suit instituted.
§ 19. Unsold land afterwards subject to sale.
§ 20. Re-valuation of unsold land; no petition required.
§ 21. Certificate of purchase.
§ 22. Statement of sales by county superintendent.
§ 23. Transcript sent to Auditor.
§ 24. Patents; certificates of sale; evidence of sale.
§ 25. Duplicates of certificates of purchase.
§ 26. Real estate taken for debt, sold by county superintendent.
§ 27. Trustees may dedicate land for streets.

SECTION 1. Section number sixteen (16) in every township granted to the State by the United States for the use of schools, and such sections and parts of section as have been or may be granted, as aforesaid, in lieu of all or part of section number sixteen (16), and also the lands which have been or may be selected and granted as aforesaid, for the use of schools, to the inhabitants of fractional townships in which there is no section number sixteen (16), or where such section shall not contain the proper proportion for the use of schools in such fractional township, shall be held as common school lands; and the provisions of this act referring to common school lands shall be deemed to apply to the lands aforesaid.

§ 2. All the business of such townships, so far as relates to common school lands, shall be transacted in that county which contains all or a greater portion of said lands.

§ 3. It shall be lawful for the trustees of schools in townships in which section number sixteen (16), or any other lands granted in lieu thereof, remain unsold or which has title to any other school lands whatsoever, to rent or lease the same for an annual rent to be paid in money to the treasurer, by a written contract made by the president and clerk, under the direction of the board, with lessee or lessees, which contract shall be filed with the records of the board, and a copy of the same transmitted to the county superintendent. In case of any default in the payment of the rent, the said board of trustees shall at once proceed to collect the same by distress, or otherwise, as may be provided by law for the collection of rents by landlords. No lease taken under the provisions of this act, shall be for a longer period than five years, except where such lands are leased for the purpose of having permanent improvements made thereon, as may be the case in cities and villages: *Provided*, that the provisions of this section shall not apply to cities having a population of over one hundred thousand (100,000) inhabitants.

§ 4. The trustees of schools of any township concerned, are hereby authorized and empowered in their corporate capacity, to sell and convey to any railroad company which may construct a railroad across any of the public school lands of such township, the right of way and necessary depot grounds. All moneys received by such trustees for any right of way or depot grounds so sold, shall be turned over by such trustees to the township treasurer of the township for the benefit of the township school fund.

§ 5. If any person shall, without being duly authorized, cut, fell, box, bore, destroy or carry away any tree, sapling or log standing or being upon any school lands, such person shall forfeit and pay, for every tree, sapling or log so felled, boxed, bored, destroyed or carried away, the sum of eight dollars ($8), which penalty shall be recovered with costs of suit, by an action of debt or assumpsit, before any justice of the peace having jurisdiction of the amount claimed, or in the county or circuit court, either in the corporate name of the board of trustees of the township to which the land belongs, or by *qui tam* action in the name of any person who will first sue for the same, one-half of the judgment for the use of the person suing and the other half for the use of the township aforesaid. When two or more persons shall be concerned in the same trespass, they shall be jointly and severally liable for the penalty herein imposed.

§6. Every trespasser upon common school lands, shall be liable to indictment, and upon conviction shall be fined in three times the amount of the injury occasioned by said trespass, and shall stand committed as in other cases of misdemeanor.

§ 7. All penalties and fines collected under the provisions of the foregoing sections shall be paid to the township treasurer, and be added to the principal of the township fund.

§ 8 When the inhabitants of any township or fractional township shall desire the sale of the common school lands of the township or fractional township, they shall present a petition to the county superintendent of the county in which the school lands of the township, or the greater part thereof, lie, for the sale thereof; which petition shall be signed by at least two-thirds of the legal voters of the township, or fractional township. The signing of the petition must be done in the presence of two adult citizens of the township, after the true meaning and purpose thereof have been explained; and, when signed, an affidavit must be affixed thereto by the two citizens witnessing the signing, in the manner aforesaid, which affidavit shall state the number of inhabitants in the township, or fractional township, of and over twenty-one years of age, and said petition, so proved, shall be delivered to the county superintendent for his action thereon: *Provided*, no whole section shall be sold in any township containing less than two hundred inhabitants; and common school lands in fractional townships may be sold when the number of inhabitants and the number of acres are in the ratio of two hundred to six hundred and forty, but not before.

§ 9. Any fractional township not having the requisite number of inhabitants to petition for the sale of the school lands therein, as provided in section 8 of this article of this act, which has not heretofore been united with any other township, for school purposes, and which does not contain a sufficient number of inhabitants to maintain a free school, is hereby attached to the adjacent congressional township having the longest territorial line bordering on such fractional township, for school purposes, and all the provisions of this act shall apply to such united townships, the same as though they were one and the same township.

§ 10. When the petition and affidavits are delivered to the county superintendent, as aforesaid, he shall notify the trustees of said township thereof, and said trustees shall immediately proceed to divide the land into tracts or lots, of such form and quantity as will produce the largest amount of money.

§ 11. After making the division required by the foregoing section, said trustees shall cause a correct plat of the same to be made, representing all divisions, with each lot numbered and defined, so that its boundaries may be forever ascertained.

§ 12. In subdividing said common school lands for sale, no lot shall contain more than 80 acres, and the division may be made into town or village lots, with roads, streets or alleys between them and through the same; and all such divisions, with all similar divisions hereafter made, are hereby declared legal, and all such roads, streets and alleys, public highways.

§ 13. After such division into lots has been made and platted, the trustees of schools shall fix a value on each lot, having regard to the terms of sale, certify to the correctness of the plat, stating the value of each lot per acre, or per lot if less than one acre, and referring to and describing the lot in the certificate, so as fully and clearly to distinguish, and identify each lot; which plats and certificate shall be delivered to the county superintendent, and shall govern him in advertising and selling such lands.

§ 14. Upon the reception by the county superintendent of the plat and certificate of valuation from the trustees, he shall proceed to advertise the said land for sale in lots as divided and laid off by said trustees, by posting notices thereof in at least six (6) public places in the county, forty days before the day of sale, describing the land and stating the time, place and terms of sale; and if any newspaper is published in said county, said advertisement shall be printed therein, for four weeks before the day of sale; if no newspaper is published in said county, then such land may be sold under the notice aforesaid, which notice may be in the following form, viz.:

### SALE OF SCHOOL LAND.

Public notice is hereby given that on the..........day of........A. D. 18...., between the hours of ten o'clock A. M. and six o'clock P. M.; the undersigned superintendent of schools of...............county, will sell at

77

public vendue to the highest bidder, at the..... .......door of the court house, in............., (or on the premises) the following described real estate, the same being a part of the school lands of township No........ range No..........., as divided and platted by the trustees of schools of said township, to-wit: (Here insert full and complete description of said premises). Said lands will be sold for cash in hand with the privilege to any purchaser of borrowing from the undersigned, the whole or any part of the amount of his bid, for not less than one nor more than five years, upon his paying interest and giving security as required in case of a loan obtained from the township school fund.

Dated this..........day of............A. D....

.............................................

*County Superintendent,*

..............*County.*

§ 15. The place of selling common school lands shall be at the court house of the county in which the lands are situated; or the trustees of schools may direct the sale to be made on the premises.

§ 16. The terms of selling common school lands shall be to the highest bidder for cash, with the privilege to each purchaser of borrowing from the county superintendent the amount or any part of the amount of his bid, for any period of not less than one year nor more than five years, upon his paying interest and giving security, as in case of money loaned by a township treasurer as provided in this act.

§ 17. Upon the day appointed for such sale, the county superintendent shall proceed to make sales as follows, viz.: He shall begin at the lowest numbered lot and proceed regularly to the highest numbered, till all are sold or offered. No lot shall be sold for less than its valuation by the trustees. Said sale shall be made between the hours of ten o'clock A. M. and six o'clock P. M., and may continue from day to day. The lots shall be cried separately, and each lot cried long enough to enable any person present to bid who desires to bid.

§ 18. Upon closing the sales each day, the purchasers shall each pay, or secure the payment of the purchase money, according to the terms of sale; or in case of his failure to do so by ten o'clock the succeeding day, the lot purchased shall again be offered at public sale, on the same terms as before, and if the valuation or more shall be bid, shall be stricken off; but if the valuation be not bid, the lot shall be set down as not sold. If the sale is or is not made, the former purchaser shall be required to pay the difference between his bid and the valuation of the lot, and in case of his failing to make such payment, the county superintendent may forthwith institute an action of debt or assumpsit in his name, as superintendent, for the use of the inhabitants of the township where the land lies, for the required sum; and upon making proof, shall be entitled to judgment, with costs of suit; which, when collected, shall be added to the principal of the township fund. If the sum claimed does not exceed two hundred dollars, the suit may be commenced before a justice of the peace; if the sum demanded exceeds two hundred dollars, then suit may be brought in the circuit court of any county wherein the party may be found.

§ 19. All lands not sold at public sale, as herein provided for, shall be subject to sale at any time thereafter, at the valuation; and the county superintendents are authorized and required, when in their power, to sell all such lands at private sale, upon the terms at which they were offered at public sale.

§ 20. In all cases where common school lands have been heretofore valued, and have remained unsold for two years, after having been offered for sale, or shall hereafter remain unsold for that length of time, after being valued and offered for sale, in conformity to this act, the trustees of schools where such lands are situated may vacate the valuation thereof by an order to be entered in book A of the county superintendent, and cause a new valuation to be made, if, in their opinion, the interests of the township will be promoted thereby. They shall make said second valuation in the same manner as the first was made, and shall deliver to the county superintendent a plat of such second valuation, with the order of vacation, to be entered, as aforesaid; whereupon, said county superintendent shall proceed to sell said lands in all respects, as if no former valuation had been made: *Provided*, that the second valuation may be made by the trustees of schools, without petition, as provided in this act for the first valuation.

§ 21. Upon the completion of every sale by the purchaser, the county superintendent shall enter the same in book B, and shall deliver to the purchaser a certificate of purchase, stating therein the name and residence of the purchaser, describing the land and the price paid therefor, which certificate shall be evidence of the facts therein stated.

§ 22. At the first regular term of the county board in each year, the county superintendent shall present to the county board of his county, a statement showing the sales of school lands made subsequent to the first regular term of the previous year, which shall be a true copy of the sale book (book B).

§ 23. The county superintendent shall, also at the time aforesaid, transmit to the Auditor of Public Accounts a full and exact transcript from book B of all the sales made subsequent to each report. The statement required to be presented to the county board shall be preserved and copied by the clerk of said board into a well-bound book kept for that purpose; and the list transmitted to the Auditor shall be filed, copied and preserved in like manner.

§ 24. Every purchaser of common school lands shall be entitled to a patent from the State, conveying and assuring the title. Patents shall be made out by the Auditor, from returns made to him by the county superintendent. They shall contain a description of the land granted, and shall be in the name of and signed by the Governor, countersigned by the Auditor, with the great seal of the State affixed thereto by the Secretary of State, and shall operate to vest in the purchaser a perfect title in fee simple. When patents are executed as herein required, the Auditor shall note on the list of sales the date of each patent, in such manner as to perpetuate the evidence of its date and delivery, and thereupon transmit the same to the county superintendent of the proper county, to be by him delivered to the patentee, his heirs or assigns upon the return of the original certificate of purchase, which certificate, when returned, shall be filed and preserved by the county superintendent; and all such patents, heretofore or hereafter so issued, by the State for school lands, or duly certified copies thereof from any record legally made, shall, after the lapse of ten years from the date of such patent, and such sale having been acquiesced in for ten years by the inhabitants of the township in which the land so conveyed may be situated, be conclusive evidence as to the legality of the sale, and that the title to such land was, at the date of the patent, legally vested in the patentee.

§ 25. Purchasers of common school lands, and their heirs and assigns, may obtain duplicate copies of their certificates of purchase and patents, upon filing affidavit with the county superintendent in respect to certificates, and with the Auditor in respect to patents, proving the loss or destruction of the originals; and such copies shall have the force and effect of originals.

§ 26. When any real estate shall have been taken for any debts due to any school fund, the title to which real estate has become vested in any county superintendent for the use of the inhabitants of one or more townships or of the county, the county superintendent may lease or sell such real estate for the benefit of such township or townships, or of the county, as pro vided for in section 37 of article III of this act, regulating the leasing and sales of lands by school trustees: *Provided*, that in case the real estate be held for the benefit of any township or townships, it shall not be sold except upon the written request of the school trustees of said township or townships. The said county superintendent is hereby authorized to execute conveyances of such real estate to the purchasers when so sold.

§ 27. The trustees of schools in any township are hereby authorized and empowered, in their corporate capacity, to lay out and dedicate to the public use, for street and highway purposes, so much of the common school lands, which is unimproved or unoccupied with buildings, as may be necessary to open or extend any street or highway which may be ordered opened or extended by the municipal authorities, which are by law empowered to open or extend streets or highways in the territory where said school lands are located: *Provided*, that said trustees of schools shall be of the opinion that the benefits to accrue from the opening or extending of said street or highway, to the remainder of said common school lands, will compensate for the strip so dedicated: *And, provided further,* that it shall not be lawful for any street or other railroad to lay down railroad tracks on any strip of the common school lands so dedicated, or use the same or any part of the common school lands for railroad or street railroad purposes, except upon the purchase or lease of the same from the proper authorities, or upon the payment to the school fund of said township of the value of such use or land taken, the same as if no street or highway had been laid out thereon, to be determined by proceedings under an act entitled "An act to provide for the exercise of the right of eminent domain," approved April 10, 1872, and all amendments thereto: *And, provided further,* that this section shall not in any way affect existing leases or contracts for the lease or purchase of common school lands.

## ARTICLE XIV.

### FINES AND FORFEITURES.

§ 1.  Paid to county superintendent.
§ 2.  Duties of state's attorneys.
§ 3.  Duties of justices of the peace.
§ 4.  Report of fines; affidavit; penalty for failure to report.

§ 5.  Penalty for failure to pay over fines collected.
§ 6.  Power of the county court to examine records of delinquent officers; penalty for failure to furnish papers, etc.

SECTION 1. All fines, penalties and forfeitures imposed or incurred in any of the courts of record, or before any justice of the peace of the State, except fines, forfeitures and penalties incurred or imposed in incorporated towns or cities for the violation of the by-laws or ordinances thereof, shall, when collected, be paid to the county superintendent of schools of the county wherein such fines, penalties or forfeitures have been imposed or incurred, and the said county superintendent of schools shall give his receipt therefor to the person from whom such fine, forfeiture or penalty was received. The said county superintendent shall annually distribute such fines, penalties or forfeitures in the same manner as the common school funds of the State are distributed.

§ 2. It shall be the duty of the state's attorneys of the several counties to enforce the collection of all fines, forfeitures and penalties imposed or incurred in the courts of record of their respective counties, and to pay the same over to the county superintendent of the county wherein the same have been imposed or incurred, retaining therefrom the fees and commissions allowed them by law.

§ 3. It shall be the duty of the justices of the peace to enforce the collection of all fines imposed by them, by any lawful means; and, when collected, the same shall be paid, by the justice collecting the same, to the county superintendent of the county in which the same was imposed.

§ 4. Clerks of courts of record, state's attorneys and all justices of the peace shall report, under oath, to the county court of their respective counties, by the first of March, annually, the amount of such fines, penalties and forfeitures imposed or incurred in their respective courts, and the amount of such fines, forfeitures and penalties collected by them, giving each article separately, and if any such officer has collected no such fines, penalties or forfeitures, he shall make affidavit to such fact, and file the same with the county superintendent. The judges of the county court shall inspect the said reports, and may hear evidence thereon, and, if found correct and truthful, shall enter an order approving such report, and that any moneys in the hands of such officers so reporting shall be paid over to the superintendent of schools. If the court shall not approve of such report, he may order a new one to be made, and, upon failure to comply with the order of the court, or to make a satisfactory report, the court may state an account and enter an order to pay over as above provided. The court, for all purposes for carrying out the provisions of this section, shall have power to examine books and papers, as provided hereinafter in section 6 of this article, and shall have power to issue subpœnas for both books and persons: *Provided*, that no report shall be approved until the court shall have given the superintendent five (5) days' notice of the same, and he shall be allowed to inspect said report, and he shall be heard by the court upon the same if he desire; and the officers charged with the collection thereof (the said clerks, State's attorneys and justices of the peace), for a failure to make such a report, shall be liable to a fine of twenty-five dollars ($25) for each offense, said fine to be recovered in a civil action, before any court, at the suit of the county superintendent of schools of the proper county.

§ 5. For a failure to pay any fine, forfeiture or penalty, on demand, to the person who is by law authorized to receive the same, the officer or person having collected the same, or having the same in his possession or control, shall forfeit and pay double the amount of such fine, penalty or forfeiture as aforesaid, to be recovered before any court having jurisdiction thereof, in a *qui tam* action, one-half to be paid to the informer, and one-half to the school fund of the proper county.

§ 6. In case that any clerk of a court of record, State's attorney or justice of the peace shall fail to make the report provided for in section 4 of this article, the county court shall have power, and it is hereby made the duty of the judge of said court, to examine all records pertaining to the office of such delinquent officer, and enforce the payment of whatever sum may be found due the school fund from such delinquent officer. For the purpose of making such examination, the said county court shall have the right to call for any paper or papers, docket, fee-book, or other record belonging to the office of such delinquent officer; and in case such delinquent officer fails or refuses to furnish such paper, docket, fee-book, or other record, for the inspection or use of such county court, he shall forfeit, and pay to the school fund, the sum of one hundred dollars ($100), to be recovered in an action of debt or assumpsit,

—6 S.

before any court of this State having jurisdiction of the actions of debt and assumpsit, and such penalty, when collected, shall be paid into the school fund of the proper county.

## ARTICLE XV.

### LIABILITY OF SCHOOL OFFICERS.

§ 1. Of trustees for failure to take action regarding the insufficiency of township securities.

§ 2. Of judges of election for failure to deliver poll-book and certificates.

§ 3. Of boards of directors for failure to deliver schedules.

§ 4. Of township treasurer for failure to perform his duties

§ 5. Of the bondsmen or legal representatives of township treasurer to turn over bonds, etc., to successor.

§ 6. Liable to indictment and imprisonment for conversion of funds.

§ 7. Trustees liable for securities of township treasurer; exception.

§ 8. Real estate of school officers holden.

§ 9. Failure of trustees to make returns of children.

§ 10. Failure of school officers to furnish statistics.

§ 11. School officers responsible for loss of funds.

§ 12. Forbidden to pervert funds to sectarian purposes.

§ 13. Interest in sale of school books, etc., forbidden.

§ 14. Penalty for excluding colored children from school.

SECTION 1. Whenever the county superintendent of schools of any county shall notify the board of trustees of any township, in writing, that the notes, bonds, mortgages, or other evidences of indebtedness which have been taken officially by the township treasurer, are not in proper form, or that the securities which the said township treasurer has taken are insufficient, it shall be the duty of the said board of trustees at once to take such action as may be necessary to save and protect the property or funds of the districts and the township; and for a failure or refusal to take such action within twenty (20) days after such notice, the members of the board, each in his individual capacity, shall be liable to a fine of not less than twenty-five (25) nor more than one hundred dollars ($100), to be recovered before any justice of the peace, on information, in the name of the People of the State of Illinois (provided such insufficiency is proven), and, when collected, the said fine shall be paid to the county superintendent of the proper county, for the use of schools. And the payment of this fine shall not relieve the board of trustees from any civil liability they may have incurred from such neglect of duty.

§ 2. If the judges of any school election called for any legal purpose shall fail or neglect to deliver a copy of the poll-book of any such election, with a certificate thereon showing the result of such election, to the officer provided by law to whom such return shall be made, within ten days after such election shall have been held, the said judges of election shall be severally liable to a penalty of not less than twenty-five dollars ($25) nor more than one hundred dollars ($100), to be recovered in the name of the People of the State of Illinois, by an action of debt before any justice of the peace of the county; which penalty, when collected, shall be paid into the school fund of the township in which such election was held.

§ 3. It shall be the duty of the board of directors of every school district in this State, to deliver to the township treasurer all teachers' schedules made and certified as required by law, and covering all time taught during the school year ending June 30th, on or before the 7th day of July, annually; and the directors shall be personally liable to the district for any and all loss sustained by it through their failure to examine and deliver to the said township treasurer all such schedules within the said time.

§ 4. For any failure or refusal to perform all the duties required of the township treasurer by law, he shall be liable to the board of trustees, upon his official bond, for all damages sustained by reason of such failure or refusal, to be recovered by action of debt by said board, in their corporate name, for the use of the proper township, before any court having jurisdiction of the amount of damages claimed; but if the said treasurer, in any such failure or refusal, acted under and in conformity to a requisition or order of said board, or a majority of them, entered upon their journal and subscribed by their president and clerk, then, in that case, the members of said board aforesaid, or those of them voting for such requisition or order aforesaid, and not the said township treasurer, shall be liable, jointly and severally, to the inhabitants of the township for all such damages, to be recovered by an action of assumpsit in a suit brought in the official name of the county superintendent of schools, for the use of the proper township: *Provided*, said treasurer shall be liable for any loss not collected by reason of the insolvency of said trustees.

§ 5. When a township treasurer shall resign or be removed, and at the expiration of his term of office, he shall pay over to his successor in office, when appointed, all money on hand, and deliver over all books, notes, bonds, mortgages, and all other securities for money, and all papers and documents of every description in which the corporation has any interest whatever; and in case of the death of the township treasurer, his securities and legal representatives shall be bound to comply with the requisitions of this section so far as the said securities and legal representatives may have the power so to do. And for any failure to comply with the requisitions of this section, the persons neglecting or refusing shall be liable to a penalty of not less than ten (10) nor more than one hundred dollars ($100), at the discretion of the court before which judgment may be obtained, to be recovered in an action of debt before any justice of the peace, for the benefit of the school fund of such township: *Provided*, that the obtaining or payment of such judgment shall in no wise discharge or diminish the obligation of the persons signing the official bond of such township treasurer.

§ 6. If any county superintendent, trustee of schools, township treasurer, director or any other person entrusted with the care, control, management or disposition of any school, college, seminary or township fund for the use of any county, township, district or school, shall convert such funds, or any part thereof, to his own use, he shall be liable to indictment; and upon conviction thereof, shall be fined in any sum not less than double the amount of money converted to his own use, and imprisoned in the county jail not less than one nor more than twelve months, at the discretion of the court.

§ 7. Trustees of schools shall be liable, jointly and severally, for the sufficiency of securities taken from township treasurers; and in case of judgment against any treasurer and his securities for or on account of any default of such treasurer on which the money shall not be made for want of sufficient property whereon to levy execution, action on the case may be maintained against said trustees, jointly and severally, and the amount not collected on said judgment shall be recovered with costs of suit from such trustees: *Provided*, that if said trustees can show, satisfactorily, that the security taken from the treasurer, as aforesaid, was, at the time of said taking, good and sufficient, they shall not be liable as' aforesaid.

§ 8. The real estate of county superintendents, of township treasurers, and all other school officers, and of the securities of each of them shall be bound for the satisfaction and payment of all claims and demands against said superintendents and treasurers, and other school officers as such from the date of issuing process against them, in actions or suits brought to recover such claims or demands until satisfaction thereof be obtained; and no sale or alienation of real estate, by any superintendent, treasurer or other officer or security aforesaid, shall defeat the lien created by this section; but all and singular such real estate held, owned or claimed, as aforesaid, shall be liable to be sold in satisfaction of any judgment which may be obtained in such actions or suits.

§ 9. Trustees of schools, or either of them, failing or refusing to make returns of children in their township according to the provisions of this act, or if either of them shall knowingly make a false return, the party so offending shall be liable to a penalty of not less than ten dollars ($10) nor more than one hundred dollars ($100), to be recovered by an action of assumpsit, before any justice of the peace of the county; which penalty, when collected, shall be added to the township school fund of the township in which said trustees reside.

§ 10. If any county superintendent, director or trustee, or either of them, or other officer whose duty it is, shall negligently or willfully fail or refuse to make, furnish or communicate the statistics and information, or shall fail to discharge the duties enjoined upon them or either of them, at the time and in the manner required by the provisions of this act, such delinquent or party offending shall be liable to a fine of not less than twenty-five dollars ($25), to be recovered before any justice of the peace at the suit of any person, on information in the name of the People of the State of Illinois, and when collected, the said fine shall be paid to the county superintendent of the proper county for the use of the school fund.

§ 11. County superintendents, trustees of schools, directors and township treasurers, or either of them, or any other officer having charge of school funds or property, shall be pecuniarily responsible for all losses sustained by any county, township or school fund, by reason of any failure on his or their part to perform the duties required of him or them by the provisions of this act; or by any rule or regulation authorized to be made by the provisions of this act; and each and every one of the officers aforesaid shall be liable for any such loss sustained as aforesaid, and the amount of such loss may be recovered in a civil action brought in any court having jurisdiction thereof, at the suit of the State of Illinois, for the use of the county, township or fund injured; the amount of the judgment obtained in such suit shall, when collected, be paid to the proper officer for the benefit of the said county, township or fund injured.

§ 12. No county, city, town, township, school district or other public corporation shall ever make any appropriation, or pay from any school fund whatever, anything in aid of any church or sectarian purpose, or to help support or sustain any school, academy, seminary, college, university or other literary or scientific institution controlled by any church or sectarian denomination whatever; nor shall any grant or donation of money, or other personal property, ever be made by any such corporation to any church or for any sectarian purpose; and any officer or other person having under his charge or direction school funds or property, who shall pervert the same in the manner forbidden in this section, shall be liable to indictment, and upon conviction thereof shall be fined in a sum not less than double the value of the property so perverted, and imprisoned in the county jail not less than one (1) nor more than twelve (12) months, at the discretion of the court.

§ 13. No teacher, state, county, township or district school officer shall be interested in the sale, proceeds or profits of any book, apparatus or furniture used, or to be used, in any school in this State with which such officer or teacher may be connected; and for offending against the provisions of this section such teacher, state, county, township or district school officer shall be liable to indictment, and upon conviction shall be fined in a sum not less than twenty-five dollars ($25) nor more than five hundred dollars ($500), and may be imprisoned in the county jail not less than one (1) month nor more than twelve (12) months, at the discretion of the court.

§ 14. Any school officer or officers, or any other person, who shall exclude or aid in the exclusion from the public schools, of any child who is entitled to the benefits of such school, on account of such child's color, shall be fined, upon conviction, in any sum not less than five dollars ($5), nor more than one hundred dollars ($100) each, for every such offense.

## ARTICLE XVI.

### MISCELLANEOUS.

Costs of suits not to be charged to school fund.
Eligibility of women to school offices.
Bonds of women holding school offices.
Colored children may not be excluded from school.
§ 5. Penalty for preventing children from attending school.
§ 6. Payment of funds to township treasurer.
§ 7. Reports and rate of taxation under special charters.

§ 8. Educational institutions to report to State Superintendent.
§ 9. Judgment and executions against boards of trustees and directors.
§ 10. No compensation allowed to trustees, directors, etc.; exemption from road labor, etc.
§ 11. School officers to hold until their successors are qualified.
§ 12. Former acts repealed.
§ 13. Emergency clause.

SECTION 1. No justice of the peace, constable, clerk of any court, sheriff or coroner shall charge any costs in any suit where any school officer, school corporation or any agent of any school fund, suing for the recovery of the same, or any interest due thereon, is plaintiff and shall be unsuccessful in such suit; nor where the costs can not be recovered from the defendant by reason of the insolvency of such defendant.

§ 2. Any woman, married or single, of the age of twenty-one years and upwards, and possessing the qualifications prescribed for the office, shall be eligible to any office under the general or special school laws of this State.

§ 3. Any woman elected or appointed to any office under the provisions of this act, before she enters upon the discharge of the duties of the office, shall qualify and give the bond required by law (if a bond is required), and such bond shall be binding upon her and her securities.

§ 4. All boards of school directors, boards of education, or school officers, whose duty it now is, or may be hereafter to provide, in their respective jurisdictions, schools for the education of all children between the ages of six and twenty-one years, are prohibited from the excluding, directly or indirectly, any such child from such school on account of the color of such child.

§ 5. Any person who shall, by threats, menace or intimidation, prevent any child entitled to attend a public school in this State from attending such school shall, upon conviction, be fined in any sum not exceeding twenty-five dollars ($25.00).

§ 6. It shall be the duty of the county treasurers, county superintendents of schools, township collectors, and all other

persons paying money into the hands of township school treasurers, for school purposes, on or before the 30th day of September of each year, to notify in writing the presidents of boards
of school trustees, and the clerks of the boards of school directors, of the amount paid into the township treasurer's hands,
and the date of payment.

§ 7. This act shall not be so construed as to repeal or
change, in any respect, any special acts in relation to schools
in cities having less than 100,000 inhabitants, or incorporated
towns, townships or districts (except that in every such city,
town, township or district the limit of taxation for educational
and building purposes shall be the same as that fixed in section
one, article eight, of this act); and except that it shall be the
duty of the several boards of education or other officers of any
city or incorporated town, township or district, having in charge
schools under the provision of any of said special acts, or of
any ordinance of any city or incorporated town, on or before
the 15th day of July preceding each session of the General Assembly of this State, or annually, if required so to do by the
State Superintendent of Public Instruction, to make out and
render a statement of all such statistics and other information
in regard to schools and the enumeration of persons, as is required to be communicated by township boards of trustees or
directors, under the provisions of this act, or so much thereof
as may be applicable to said city or incorporated town, to the
county superintendent of the county where such city or incorporated town is situated, or of the county in which the larger
part of such city or incorporated town is situated; nor shall it
be lawful for the county superintendent, or any other officer or
person to pay over any portion of the common school fund to
any local treasurer, school agent, clerk, board of education, or
other officer or person of any township, city or incorporated
town, unless a report of the number of persons and other statistics relative to schools, and a statement of such other information as is required by the board of trustees or of directors,
as aforesaid, and of other school officers and teachers, under the
provisions of this act, shall have been filed at the time or times
aforesaid, specified in this section, with the superintendent of
the proper county, as aforesaid. [As amended by act approved
and in force March 31, 1891.]

§ 8. It shall be the duty of the president, principal, or other
proper officer of every organized university, college, seminary,
academy, or other literary institution, heretofore incorporated,
or hereafter to be incorporated in this State, to make out, or
cause to be made out and forwarded to the office of the State
Superintendent of Public Instruction, on or before the first day
of August in each year, a report setting forth the amount and
estimated value of real estate owned by the corporation, the
amount of other-funds and endowments, and the yearly income
from all sources, the number of instructors, the number of
students in the different classes, the studies pursued and the

books used, the course of instruction, the terms of tuition, and such other matters as may be specially requested by said Superintendent, or as may be deemed proper by the president or principal of such institution to enable the Superintendent of Public Instruction to lay before the Legislature a fair and full exhibit of the affairs and conditions of said institutions, and of the educational resources of the State.

§ 9. If judgment shall be obtained against any township board of trustees or school directors, the party entitled to the benefit of such judgment may have execution therefor, as follows, to-wit: It shall be lawful for the court in which such judgment shall be obtained, or to which such judgment may be removed by transcript or appeal from a justice of the peace, or other court, to issue thence a writ commanding the directors, trustees and treasurer of such township, to cause the amount thereof, with interest and costs, to be paid to the party entitled to the benefit of such judgment; out of any moneys unappropriated of said township or district, or if there be no such moneys, out of the first moneys applicable to the payment of the kind of services or indebtedness for which such judgment shall be obtained, which shall be received for the use of such township or district and to enforce obedience to such writ by attachment, or by mandamus, requiring such board to levy a tax for the payment of such judgment; and all legal processes, as well as writs to enforce payment, shall be served either on the president or clerk of the board.

§ 10. Trustees of schools, school directors, members of boards of education, or other school officers performing like duties, shall receive no pecuniary compensation, but they shall be exempt from road labor and from military duty during their term of office.

§ 11. All school officers elected in pursuance of any general law now in force shall hold their respective offices until their successors are elected and qualified under the provisions of this act.

§ 12. "An Act to establish and maintain a system of free schools," approved April 1, 1872; "An Act to protect colored children in their rights to attend public schools," approved March 24, 1874; "An Act to amend section fifty (50) of an act entitled 'An Act to establish and maintain a system of free schools,' approved April 1, 1872," approved March 30, 1874; "An Act to amend sections 24 and 33 of an act entitled 'An Act to establish and maintain a system of free schools,' approved April 1, 1872," approved May 23, 1877; "An Act to amend section 47 of an act to establish and maintain a system of free schools, approved April 1, 1872," approved May 11, 1877; "An act regulating the renting and sale of school lands," approved May 25, 1877; "An act to amend section 33 of an act entitled 'An act to amend sections 24 and 33 of an act entitled "An Act to establish and maintain a system of free

89

schools,'' ' approved April 1, 1872, approved May 23, 1877; in force July 1, 1877," approved May 31, 1879; "An Act to amend an act entitled 'An Act to establish and maintain a sys· tem of free schools,' approved April 1, 1872, and section forty-seven (47) of said act as amended by an act approved May 11. 1877,'' approved June 3, 1879; "An Act to amend sections eleven (11), twenty·seven (27), thirty·three (33), thirty-four (34), forty·eight (48), fifty·three (53), fifty·four (54) and fifty-seven (57) of an act entitled 'An Act to establish and maintain a system of free schools,' approved April 1, 1872, and in force July 1, 1872, and amended by an act approved June 3, 1879, and in force July 1, 1879," approved May 31, 1881; "An Act to amend section fifty one (51) of an act entitled 'An Act to establish and maintain a system of free schools,' approved April 1, 1872, in force July 1, 1872, and amended by an act approved June 3, 1879, in force July 1, 1879," approved June 23, 1883; "An Act regulating the loaning of school funds," approved and in force March 20, 1883; "An Act to amend sections thirteen (13), twenty (20) and seventy-one (71) of an act entitled 'An Act to establish and maintain a system of free schools,' approved April 1, 1872, and in force July 1, 1872, and amended by an act approved June 3, 1879," approved June 26, 1885; "An Act to amend sections fifty-seven (57) and fifty-eight (58) of an act entitled 'An Act to establish and maintain a system of free schools,' approved April 1, 1872, and amended by an act approved April 1, 1872, and amended by an act approved June 3, 1879, and in force July 1, 1879, and further amended by an act approved May 31, 1881, and in force July 1, 1881," approved June 30, 1885; "An Act to amend section one (1) of an act entitled 'An Act regulating the renting and sale of school lands,' approved May 25, 1877, in force July 1, 1877," approved June 29, 1885; "An Act to amend section thirty-three (33) of an Act entitled 'An Act to establish and maintain a system of free schools,' approved April 1, 1872, in force July 1, 1872, as amended by an act approved May 23, 1877, in force July 1, 1877, as amended by act approved June 3, 1879, in force July 1, 1879, as amended by act approved May 31, 1881, in force July 1, 1881," approved June 4, 1877; "An Act to provide for the election of presidents of boards of education in school dis-tricts," approved June 17, 1887; "An Act to empower trustees of schools to lay out and dedicate common school lands for street and highway purposes," approved June 3, 1887; "An Act to regulate the attendance of teachers upon teachers' institutes," approved June 14, 1887; "An Act to empower township trustees to sell and convey right of way and depot grounds for the use of railroads crossing school lands," approved April 13, 1875; "An Act to regulate the payment of moneys into the hands of township school treasurers," approved May 30, 1881; and all other acts and parts of acts inconsistent with this act, and all general school laws in this State, are hereby repealed.

§ 13. Whereas, an emergency exists, requiring this act to take immediate effect, therefore be it enacted that this act shall take effect from and after its passage.

APPROVED May 21, 1889.

## ADDITIONAL FACTS PERTAINING TO THE PUBLIC SCHOOLS AND TO SCHOOL OFFICERS.

### MEMBERS OF THE BOARD OF EDUCATION APPOINTED.

*An Act to provide for the appointment of School Directors and members of the Board of Education, in certain cases, approved May 29, 1879, in force July 1, 1879.*

SECTION 1. *Be it enacted by the People of the State of Illinois, represented in the General Assembly:* That in all cases whereby [where, by] the provisions of any general or special law of this State heretofore passed, the members of the common council of any city having been made *ex officio* school directors, or members of the board of education in and for the school district of which the said city shall constitute the whole or a part, the said school directors or members of the board of education shall hereafter be appointed as hereinafter provided.

§ 2. It shall be the duty of the mayor of said city, at the first regular meeting of the city council after each annual municipal election, and after his installation into office, to nominate and place before the council, for confirmation as school directors or members of the board of education, as the case may be, one person from each ward of said city to serve for two years, and one person from the city at large to serve for one year, and if the persons so appointed shall be confirmed by a majority vote of the city council, to be entered of record, the persons so appointed, together with such persons theretofore appointed under the provisions of the act, to which this is an amendment, whose terms of service shall not expire within one year, shall constitute the board of education or school directors for such district: *Provided,* that the person appointed from the city at large for one year shall be president of said board of education or school directors, but shall have no vote in such board excepting in case of a tie: *And, provided, further,* that the term of office of all persons heretofore appointed under the provisions of the act to which this is an amendment, whose term of office expires within one year, shall terminate at the first regular meeting of the city council after the annual meeting, and upon the appointment and confirmation of their successors. [As amended by act approved and in force May 28, 1889.

§ 3. The said persons shall, as soon as practicable after their appointment, organize by electing one of their number secretary, who shall hold his office for one year. All rights, powers and duties heretofore exercised by and devolved upon the members of the city council, as *ex officio* members of the board of education, or school directors, shall devolve upon and be exercised by the members of the board of education and school directors appointed under the provisions of this act. [As amended by act approved and in force May 28, 1889.

§ 4. In all school districts to which this act shall apply, the boards of education or school directors shall annually, before the first day of August, certify to the city council, under the hands and seals of the president and secretary of the board, the amount of money required to be raised by taxation for school purposes in said district for the ensuing year, and the said city council shall thereupon cause the said amount to be levied and collected in the same manner now provided by law for the levy and collection of taxes for school purposes in such district, but the amount to be so levied and collected shall not exceed the amount now allowed to be collected for school purposes by the general school laws of this State; and when such taxes have been collected and paid over to the treasurer of such city or school district, as may be provided by the terms of the act under which such district has been organized, such funds shall be paid out only on the order of the board of education or the school directors, signed by the president and secretary of such board.

APPROVED May 29, 1879.

LIBRARY
OF THE
UNIVERSITY
OF CALIFORNIA

AN ACT *relating to the study of Physiology and Hygiene in the Public Schools.*

SECTION 1. *Be it enacted by the People of the State of Illinois, represented in the General Assembly:* That the proper legal school authorities shall have power, and it shall be their duty, to have all pupils of suitable age in schools of Illinois, supported by public money or under State control, instructed in physiology and hygiene, with special reference to the effects of alcoholic beverages, stimulants and narcotics on the human system.

§ 2. No certificate shall be granted to any person to teach in the public schools of Illinois, after July, 1890, who has not passed a satisfactory examination in physiology and hygiene, with special reference to the effects of alcoholic beverages, stimulants and narcotics on the human system.

APPROVED June 1, 1889.

COMPENSATION OF JUDGES AND CLERKS OF ELECTION IN CER-
TAIN CASES.*

*An act to provide for the compensation of Judges and Clerks
of Election at elections at which Trustees of Schools and
School Directors are elected under the provisions of an act
entitled "An act to regulate the holding of elections and declaring the result thereof in cities, villages and incorporated
towns in this State," approved June 19, 1885.*

SECTION 1.  *Be it enacted by the People of the State of Illinois, represented in the General Assembly:*  That at all elections
held under the provisions of an act entitled "An Act to regulate
the holding of elections and declaring the result thereof in cities,
villages, and incorporated towns in this State," approved June
19, 1885, and those amendatory and supplemental thereto, at
which any trustee of school may have been heretofore or shall
hereafter be elected, the expenses of such election shall be paid
out of the treasury of such city, village and incorporated town.

§ 2.  That all elections held under the provisions of said acts,
at which a school director is elected, the expenses of such election shall be paid out of any funds belonging or appertaining
to the district for which such director is elected.

§ 3.  The corporate authorities of cities, villages, incorporated towns and school districts are hereby authorized and
empowered to levy taxes for the purpose of paying such election
expenses

APPROVED June 3, 1889.

---

ELECTION OF BOARDS OF EDUCATION IN
CERTAIN CASES.

§ 1. Cities, towns and townships, in which schools are managed under special acts, may elect boards of education.
§ 2. Question to be submitted to vote, upon petition of 50 voters.
§ 3. Repeals all acts in conflict.
§ 4. Emergency.

AN ACT *to give cities, incorporated towns, townships and districts in which free schools are now managed under special
acts, authority to elect boards of education having the same
powers as boards of education now elected under the general
free school laws of this State.*

SECTION 1.  *Be it enacted by the People of the State of Illinois, represented in the General Assembly:*  That any city, incorporated town, township or district having a population of

---

* This relates to the judges and clerks of elections appointed by the board of election commissioners, and not to the officers of school elections generally.

not less than one thousand and not over twenty thousand inhabitants, in which free schools are now managed under any special act, may, by vote of its electors, determine to elect, instead of the directors or other governing or managing board, now provided for by such special act, a board of education which shall be elected at the time and in the manner and have the powers now conferred by law upon boards of education of districts not governed by any special act.

§ 2. Upon petition of fifty voters of such city, town, township or district, presented to the board having the control and management of schools in such city, town, township or district, it shall be the duty of such board, at the next ensuing election to be held in such city, town, township or district, to cause to be submitted to the voters thereof, giving not less than fifteen days' notice thereof, by posting not less than five notices in the most public places in such city, town, township or district, the question of "electing a board of education having the powers conferred upon such boards in districts organized under the free school laws," which notice may be in the following form, to-wit:

Public notice is hereby given that on the........day of............., A. D........, an election will be held at................, between the hours of........ m. and........m. of said day, for the purpose of deciding the question of "electing a board of education having the powers conferred upon such boards in districts organized under the free school law."

If it shall appear, upon a canvass of the returns of such election, that a majority of the votes cast at such election are "for electing a board of education having the powers conferred upon such boards in districts organized under the free school law," then at the time of the next regular election for boards of education under the free school law, there shall be elected a board of education for such district; and should there not be sufficient time to give the notice required by law for such election, then such election may be held on any Saturday thereafter, but all subsequent elections shall be held at the time provided by the free school law.

§ 3. All acts and parts of acts in conflict with this act are hereby repealed.

§ 4. Whereas, an emergency exists requiring this act to take immediate effect, therefore be it enacted that this act shall be in force from and after its passage.

APPROVED June 2, 1891.

# CHILD LABOR.

### EMPLOYMENT OF CHILDREN UNDER 13 YEARS OF AGE PROHIBITED.

§ 1. Prohibits any person, firm or corporation from employing any child under 13 years of age, except as provided in this act.
§ 2. Certificate of the school board authorizing employment.

§ 3. No certificate shall be issued unless the child has attended school at least 8 weeks in the current school year.
§ 4. No child shall be employed for more than one day without such certificate.
§ 5. Penalties for violation of this act.

AN ACT *to prevent child labor.*

SECTION 1. *Be it enacted by the People of the State of Illinois, represented in the General Assembly:* That it shall be unlawful for any person, firm or corporation to employ or hire any child under thirteen years of age except as hereinafter provided.

§ 2. In case it shall be made to appear to the board of education or of school directors that the labor or services of any child constitutes and is the means of support of an aged or infirm relative, and that such relative is, in whole or in part, dependent upon such child, then the board of education or school directors shall issue to such child a certificate authorizing the employment of such child; such certificate shall state the name, residence and age of such child, and a record thereof shall be kept by the board of education or school directors in a book kept for that purpose.

§ 3. No such certificate shall be granted to any child unless it shall be shown to the board of education or school directors [of the district] in which such child resides, that such child has attended some public or private day school for at least eight (8) weeks in the current school year.

§ 4. No person, firm or corporation shall employ any child under the age of thirteen years, in any store, shop, factory or manufacturing establishment, by the day, or any period of time greater than one day, unless such certificate be furnished, nor shall he permit any such child to work in his employ without such certificate. He or they shall be authorized to retain the certificate of any such child employed by him, which shall be evidence admissible in any court.

§ 5. Any person, firm or corporation who violates the provisions of this act, and any father, guardian or person having control of any child under the age of thirteen years, who willingly permits or consents to the employment of such child without such certificate as is prescribed by section three of this act shall, for every offense, be fined in a sum not less than ten nor more than fifty dollars, for the use of public schools of the city or district in which such child resides. And every day of the employment of any such child shall be deemed a separate offense.

APPROVED June 17, 1891.

# WOMEN MAY VOTE AT SCHOOL ELECTIONS.

§ 1. Confers the right of suffrage upon women 21 years of age and over who may vote at elections for school officers. Registration.

§ 2. Shall be permitted to vote for school officers at any election. Ballots, at general elections, to be put into separate boxes.

AN ACT *to entitle women to vote at any election held for the purpose of choosing any officer under the general or special school laws of this State.*

SECTION 1. *Be it enacted by the People of the State of Illinois, represented in the General Assembly:* Any woman of the age of twenty-one years and upwards, belonging to either of the classes mentioned in article 7 of the Constitution of the State of Illinois, who shall have resided in this State one year, in the county ninety days, and in the election district thirty days preceding any election held for the purpose of choosing any officer of schools under the general or special school laws of this State, shall be entitled to vote at such election in the school district of which she shall at the time have been for thirty days a resident: *Provided,* any woman so desirous of voting at any such election shall have been registered in the same manner as is provided for the registration of male voters.

§ 2. Whenever the election of public school officers shall occur at the same election at which other public officers are elected, the ballot offered by any woman entitled to vote under this act shall not contain the name of any person to be voted for at such election, except such officers of public schools, and such ballots shall all be deposited in a separate ballot-box, but canvassed with other ballots cast for school officers at such election.

APPROVED June 19, 1891.

# EXISTING INDEBTEDNESS.

§ 1. Authorizes the directors of any school district, created by special act, the limits of which are co-extensive with a city, to assume and pay any existing indebtedness.

AN ACT *to allow directors of schools under special laws to assume and provide for indebtedness heretofore created by the authorities of a city for school purposes.*

SECTION 1. *Be it enacted by the People of the State of Illinois, represented in the General Assembly:* That whenever any city in this State is by special law made a school district, or whenever any school district created by special law shall be coterminous with any city, the directors of such district shall have the power, at the request of the city council, to assume and provide for, by borrowing and taxation, any indebtedness now existing, created by the authorities of the city for school purposes.

APPROVED June 22, 1891.

# COMPULSORY ATTENDANCE.

§ 1. Requires that children between the ages of 7 and 14 years shall attend school at least 16 weeks in each year unless exempt.

§ 2. Penalties for violation of this act.

§ 3. Appointment of truant officers. Hearing of charges for non-attendance.

§ 4. Recovery of fines and penalties.

§ 5. Penalties for evasion of this act.

An ACT concerning the education of children.

SECTION 1. Be it enacted by the People of the State of Illinois, represented in the General Assembly· That every person having control of any child between the ages of seven (7) and fourteen (14) years, shall annually cause such child to attend for at least sixteen (16) weeeks, twelve weeks of which attendance shall be consecutive, some public or private day school: Provided, that this act shall not apply in any case where the child has been or is being otherwise instructed for a like period of time in the elementary branches of education, or whose physical or mental condition renders his or her attendance impracticable or inexpedient, or who is excused for sufficient reasons by any competent court of record.

§ 2.. For every willful neglect of such duty as prescribed by section one (1) of this act, the person so offending shall forfeit to the use of the public schools of the city, town or district in which such child resides, a sum not less than one dollar ($1) nor more than twenty dollars ($20), and costs of suit.

§ 3. The board of education in cities, towns, villages and school districts, and the board of school directors in school districts may, at their discretion, appoint one or more proper persons, whose duty it shall be to report all violations of this act in writing to such board of education or board of directors, whose duty it shall be, when in their opinion the evidence renders such action necessary, to notify in writing the parent or guardian that such complaint has been made, and if cause be not shown within five (5) days, to at once proceed against the responsible person as is hereby provided. It shall also be the duty of said board of education in cities, towns, villages and school districts and boards of school directors in school districts, to appoint one of their number, who shall be a discreet and proper person, whose duty it shall be to hear excuses and reasons of parents or guardians for the non-attendance of children at school and to report in writing to said boards of education or boards of directors at the next regular or special meeting the names, ages and postoffice addresses of all persons prosecuted under the provisions of this act. The persons appointed as such officers shall be entitled to such compensation for services under this act as shall be determined by the boards appointing them, and which compensation shall be paid out of the distributable school fund.

§ 4. Any fine and penalty mentioned in this act may be sued for and recovered before any court of record or justice of the peace of the proper county in the name of the People of the State of Illinois for the use of the public schools of the city, town, village or district in which said child resides.

§ 5. Any person having control of a child, who, with intent to evade the provisions of this act, shall make a willful[ly] false statement concerning the age of such child or the time such child has attended school, shall for such offense forfeit a sum of not less than $3 nor more than $20, for the use of pubschools for such city, town, village or district.

APPROVED June 19, 1893.

## INSPECTORS ELECTED UNDER CERTAIN SPECIAL ACTS.

§ 1. Certain districts, containing over 20,000 and less than 100,000 inhabitants, having special · charters, though divided for the election of school inspectors, are made undivided districts with added powers for the control and management of schools.

§ 2. Moneys raised by taxation, how drawn and applied.

§ 3. Record of the proceedings of boards of Inspectors.

§ 4. Emergency.

AN ACT *extending the powers of boards of school inspectors elected under certain special acts*

SECTION 1. *Be it enacted by the People of the State of Illinois, represented in the General Assembly:* That in all cities in this State having over 20,000 and less than 100,000 inhabitants whose schools are now operated under special law, and where, by such special law, territory outside of the city limits is added to the territory within the city for school purposes, and where such school district or districts is not co-extensive with the township in which such city is situated, and where, by such special law, boards of school inspectors consisting of six members (three in each of two districts) are elected, the provisions of any such special law dividing such territory into two districts shall be held to be only for the purpose of electing members of the board of school inspectors, and for all other purposes the territory in two such districts shall be held to be included in one school organization, and the board of school inspectors, in addition to the other powers given by such special law, and general school laws, shall have power to employ teachers, janitors and such other employés as such board shall deem necessary, and to fix the amount of their conpensation; to repair and to improve school houses and to furnish them with the necessary supplies, fixtures, apparatus, libraries and fuel, and it shall be the duty of such board to take the entire supervision and control of the schools in such district or districts.

§ 2. All money necessary for the purposes mentioned in section one of this act shall be raised as now provided by law, not to exceed the amount by law limited, and shall be held by the treasurer as a special fund for school purposes, subject to the order of school inspectors, upon warrants to be counter-signed by the mayor and city clerk.

—7 S.

98

§ 3. The said board shall provide well-bound books at the
expense of the school tax fund, in which shall be kept a faithful record of all of its proceedings. The yeas and nays shall
be taken and entered on the record of the proceedings of the
board upon all questions involving the expenditure of money.

§ 4. Whereas, an emergency exists, therefore this act shall
take effect and be in force from and after its passage.

APPROVED June 19, 1893.


## SCHOOL INSPECTORS.

§ 1. Increasing number of school inspectors, | § 2. Emergency.
elected under special acts; from six to
seven members.

AN ACT *increasing the number of school inspectors, elected under
special acts, from six to seven members.*

SECTION 1. *Be it enacted by the People of the State of Illinois, represented in the General Assembly:* That in all cities in
this State having over 10,000 and less than 100,000 inhabitants,
whose schools are now operated under special law, and where,
by such special law, boards of school inspectors consisting of
six members (three in each of two districts) are elected, such
board shall hereafter consist of seven members; and at the time
other members of such boards are elected in April, 1895, and
each three years thereafter, such additional member shall be
elected for a term of three years, by all the voters entitled to
vote at school elections of the entire school territory embraced
in said two districts; and whenever such additional member is
to be elected, he shall be designated and voted for as "member of board of school inspectors at large."

§ 2. Whereas, an emergency exists, therefore this act shall
take effect and be in force from and after its passage.

APPROVED March 6, 1895.


## KINDERGARTEN SCHOOLS.

§ 1. School districts, upon authorization by | § 2. Teachers' certificates.
a majority of votes cast at an elec-
tion for that purpose, to establish kindergarten schools.

AN ACT *authorizing school districts managed by boards of education and directors to establish and maintain kindergarten
schools. Approved April 17, 1895, in force July 1, 1895.*

SECTION 1. *Be it enacted by the People of the State of Illinois,
represented in the General Assembly:* That in addition to other
grades or departments now established and maintained in the
public schools of the State, any school district managed by a
board of education or a board of directors is hereby empowered,
when authorized by a majority of all the votes cast at an election for that purpose, such election to be called and held in

99

accordance with the provisions of Article IX of an act entitled "An act to establish and maintain a system of free schools," approved and in force May 21, 1889, to establish in connection with the public schools of such district, a kindergarten or kindergartens for the instruction of children between the ages of four and six years, to be paid for in the same manner as other grades and departments now established and maintained in the public schools of such district. No money accruing to such district from the school tax fund of the State shall be used to defray the tuition or other expenses of such kindergarten, but the same shall be defrayed from the local tax and the special school revenue of said district.

§ 2. All teachers in kindergartens established under this act shall hold a certificate issued as provided by law, certifying that the holder thereof has been examined upon kindergarten principles, and is competent to teach the same.

APPROVED April 17, 1895.

## TEACHERS' PENSION AND RETIREMENT FUND.

§ 1. Teachers and employés' pension and retirement fund in certain cities—How created.
§ 2. Board of trustees—Administration and investment of fund.
§ 3. Retirement.
§ 4. Annuity.
§ 5. Powers of trustee.
§ 6. Special fund — How created—How and when drawn.
§ 7. Custodian of fund.
§ 8. Removals — Contributions refunded to teachers.

AN ACT *to provide for the formation and disbursement of a public school teachers and public school employés' pension and retirement fund in cities having a population exceeding one hundred thousand inhabitants.*

SECTION 1. *Be it enacted by the People in the State of Illinois represented in the General Assembly:* That the board of education in cities having a population exceeding one hundred thousand inhabitants, shall have power, and it shall be the duty of said board, to create a public school teachers and public school employés' pension and retirement fund, and for that purpose set apart the following moneys, to-wit:

1. An amount not exceeding one per cent. per annum of the respective salaries paid to teachers and school employés elected by such board of education, which amount shall be deducted in equal installments from said salaries at the regular times for the payment of such salaries.

2. All moneys received from donations, legacies, gifts, bequests, or otherwise, on account of said fund.

3. All moneys which may be derived from any and all sources: *Provided, however,* that no taxes shall ever be levied or an appropriation of public money be made for said fund except as herein provided.

§ 2. The board of education together with the superintendent of schools, and two representatives to be selected annually by the teachers and employés of the public schools under control of said board shall form a board of trustees, a majority of whom shall determine the amount to be deducted from the salaries paid to teachers and employés as aforesaid, and shall have charge of, and administer said fund, and shall have power to invest the same as shall be deemed most beneficial to said fund, in the same manner and subject to the same terms and conditions as township treasurers are permitted to invest school funds in article four (4) of an act entitled "An act to establish and maintain a system of free schools," in force May 4, 1889, and shall have power to make payments from said fund of annuities granted in pursuance of this act, and shall from time to time make and establish such rules and regulations for the administration of said fund as they shall deem best.

§ 3. Said board of education shall have power, by a majority vote of all its members to retire any female teacher or other female school employé who shall have taught in public schools or rendered service therein for a period aggregating twenty years; and any male teacher or male school employé who shall have taught or rendered service for a period aggregating twenty-five years, and such teacher or school employé also shall have the right after said term of service to retire and become a beneficiary under this act: *Provided, however*, that three-fifths of said term of service shall have been rendered by said beneficiary within the limits of the municipality where said board of education has jurisdiction.

§ 4. Each teacher and school employé so retired or retiring shall thereafter be entitled to receive as an annuity one-half of the annual salary paid to said teacher or employé at the date of such retirement, said annuity to be paid monthly during the school year: *Provided, however*, that such annuity shall not exceed the sum of six hundred dollars ($600), which shall be paid by said board of education out of the fund created in accordance with this act in the manner provided by law for the payment of salaries.

§ 5. Said board of trustees is hereby given the power to use both the principal and the income of said fund for the payment of annuities hereinbefore mentioned, and shall have power to reduce, from time to time, the amount of all annuities: *Provided*, that such reduction shall be at the same rate in all cases

§ 6. The president and secretary of such board of education shall certify monthly to the city treasurer all amounts deducted from the salaries of teachers, special teachers, principals and employés of the board of education in accordance with the provisions of this act, which amounts as well as all other moneys contributed to said fund, shall be set apart and held by said treasurer as a special fund for the purposes hereinbefore specified, subject to the order of said board of education, superintendent of schools, and two representatives, as aforesaid, and shall be paid out upon warrants signed by the president and secretary of said board of education.

§ 7. The city treasurer shall be custodian of said pension fund, and shall secure and safely kéep the same subject to the control and direction of said board of trustees, and shall keep his books and accounts concerning said fund in such manner as may be prescribed by the said board. And said books and accounts shall always be subject to the inspection of the said board or any member thereof.

The treasurer shall, within ten days after his election or appointment, execute a bond to the city, with good and sufficient securities, in such penal sum as the said board shall direct, to be approved by the said board, conditioned for the faithful performance of the duties of his office, and that he will safely keep, and well and truly account for all moneys and profits which may come into his hands as such treasurer, and that on the expiration of his term of office he will surrender and deliver over to his successor all unexpended moneys and all property which may have come into his hand as treasurer of such fund. Such bond shall be filed in the office of the clerk of such city, and in case of a breach of the same or the conditions thereof, suit may be brought on the same in the name of said city for the use of said board of trustees or of any person or persons injured by such breach.

§ 8. No teacher or other school employé who has been or who shall have been elected by said board of education shall be removed or discharged except for cause upon written charges, which shall be investigated and determined by the said board of education whose action and decision in the matter shall be final.

If at any time a teacher or school employé who is willing to continue is not re-employed or is discharged before the time when he or she would under the provisions of this act be entitled to a pension, then such teacher or school employé shall be paid back at once all the money, with interest, he or she may have contributed under the law.

APPROVED May 21, 1895.

# UNITED STATES FLAGS TO BE PLACED ON SCHOOL HOUSES.

§ 1. To be upon all public school houses or within the school grounds.

§ 2. Expenses—How paid.
§ 3. Penalty.

AN ACT *to require the United States flag to be placed upon all public buildings in Illinois, or upon a flag pole erected within the school grounds surrounding such school buildings. Became a law June 26, 1895. In force July 1, 1895.*

SECTION 1. *Be it enacted by the People of the State of Illinois, represented in the General Assembly:* That the directors or board of education of every school district in the State of Illinois shall have power, and it is hereby made their duty, to cause to be erected and to keep in repair upon all public school houses, or within the school grounds surrounding such public school buildings which may be in their respective school districts, a good and sufficient flag-staff or pole, together with all necessary adjustments, and that they shall provide a United States flag of suitable proportions, which shall be floated from such flag staff or pole during the school hours of such days as the school may be in session, and as a majority of the pupils attending said school may determine: *Provided,* that the flag shall not be hoisted during any day when a violent storm or inclement weather would destroy or materially injure such flag.

§ 2. Such flag-staff or pole, adjustments and repairs and all necessary flags shall be paid for from any school moneys not otherwise appropriated, which may be in the hands of the township treasurer for the use of any school district in which such expenditures have been made.

§ 3. Any person or persons who shall willfully injure, deface or destroy any flag, flag-staff or pole, or adjustments attached thereto, erected and arranged for the purpose of carrying out the requirements of this act, shall be deemed guilty of a misdemeanor, and upon conviction shall be fined not less than one (1) dollar nor more than fifteen (15) dollars.

This bill, having remained with the Governor for the period of ten days (Sundays excepted) after the adjournment of the General Assembly, and he not having filed it with his objections thereto in the office of the Secretary of State, it becomes a law in like manner as if he had signed it. Witness my hand this 26th day of June, A. D. 1895.

W. H. HINRICHSEN,
Secretary of State.

# UNITED STATES FLAGS TO BE PLACED ON PUBLIC BUILDINGS.

§ 1. On school houses, colleges and educational institutions.
§ 2. County boards to provide flags.
§ 3. On penal, reformatory and State charitable institutions.

§ 4. Penalty.
§ 5. Prosecutions under this act.

AN ACT *to provide for placing United States national flags on school houses, court houses and other public buildings in this State. Became a law June 26, 1895. In force July 1, 1895.*

SECTION 1. Be it enacted by the People of the State of Illinois, represented in the General Assembly: That it shall be the duty of all school directors and boards of education of all public schools in the State, and trustees and boards of directors of all colleges and educational institutions of every description in this State, whether State, county, municipal, district, sectarian or private, to provide United States' national flags of not less than four by eight feet in size, and cause the same to be unfurled and kept floating from a suitable flag-staff to be placed on the top of all public school houses, college buildings, and all buildings used for educational purposes in this State, whether the same be conducted by the State, or by county, township, municipal, district, sectarian, corporation or private authority, on each and every day when such schools, colleges and educational institutions are in session, from nine o'clock a. m. to four o'clock p. m., in each and every year.

§ 2. It shall be the duty of the board of supervisors in counties under township organization, and the board of commissioners in counties not under township organization, to provide United States national flags of not less than four by eight feet in size, to be unfurled and kept floating from a suitable flag-staff to be placed on the top of the court house in their respective counties, and it is hereby made the duty of the sheriff of each and every county in the State to see that the flag so provided shall be hoisted on its flag-staff above the court house and kept floating from eight o'clock a. m. to five o'clock p. m. on each and every day of the year.

§ 3. The commissioners and trustees of all penal and reformatory and State charitable institutions of this State shall provide United States' national flags of not less than ten by twenty feet in size, and cause the same to. be unfurled and kept floating above the said penal and reformatory and State charitable institutions or on a suitable flag-pole in each and every day in the year, from eight o'clock a. m. to five o'clock p. m.: *Provided*, that the flags used by any and all of the State institutions, as provided for in this act, shall be paid for out of the funds appropriated for the running expenses of said institutions, the same as other necessary supplies are bought and paid for: *And, provided further*, that flags for use over public school buildings and court houses are hereby declared to be necessary supplies and may be paid for out of the public funds of the respective school districts and counties.

§ 4. If any of the persons named in this act, whose duty it shall be to provide flags for and have the same placed in position over the several buildings, as provided for in this act, shall refuse or neglect to so provide flags and have them placed in position as required by this act; or if the sheriff of any county in this State shall refuse or neglect to place the flag so provided in position over the court house of the county in which he is sheriff, shall, each and every one of them, be deemed guilty of a misdemeanor, and on conviction thereof be fined not less than three nor more than ten dollars and costs of suit for each and every day that they shall so neglect or refuse to comply with the provisions of this act.

§ 5. Prosecutions under this act shall be by complaint or information, and be tried by any court of competent jurisdiction under the same rules as other misdemeanors: *Provided,* that fines collected under this act shall be paid into the school fund of the district and into the county treasury of the county wherein this act has been violated: *And, provided, further,* that States' Attorneys shall be entitled to a fee of five dollars for each conviction under this act, to be collected as part of the costs of the suit; except where an appeal is taken from the justice's court to county or circuit court, then in that case the State's Attorney shall be entitled to ten dollars for each conviction, to be collected as part of the costs of the suit.

---

This bill, having remained with the Governor for a period of ten days (Sundays excepted) after the adjournment of the General Assembly, and he not having filed it with his objections thereto in the office of the Secretary of State, it becomes a law in like manner as if he had signed it. Witness my hand this 26th day of June, A. D. 1895.

W. H. HINRICHSEN,
*Secretary of State.*

# APPENDIX.

[Containing acts establishing State Normal Schools, providing for County Normal Schools and providing for State Scholarships in the University of Illinois.]

CENTRAL ILLINOIS STATE NORMAL UNIVERSITY, NORMAL.

AN ACT *for the establishment and maintenance of a Normal University.*

SECTION 1. *Be it enacted by the People of the State of Illinois, represented in the General Assembly:* That C. B. Denio, of Jo Daviess county, Simeon Wright, of Lee county, Daniel Wilkins, of McLean county, C. E. Hovey, of Peoria county, George P. Rex, of Pike county, Samuel W. Moulton, of Shelby county, John Gillespie, of Jasper county, George Bunsen, of St. Clair county, Wesley Sloan of Pope county, Ninian W. Edwards, of Sangamon county, John Eden, of Moultrie county. Flavel Mosley, of Cook county, William H. Wells, of Cook county, Albert R. Shannon, of White county, and the Superintendent of Public Instruction, *ex-officio,* with their associates, who shall be elected as herein provided, and their successors are hereby created a body corporate and politic, to be styled. "The Board of Education of the State of Illinois," and by that name and style shall have perpetual succession, and have power to contract and be contracted with, to sue and be sued, to plead and be impleaded, to acquire, hold and convey real and personal property; to have and use a common seal, and to alter the same at pleasure; to make and establish by-laws and alter or repeal the same as they shall deem necessary for the government of the normal university hereby authorized to be established, or any of its departments. officers, students or employés, not in conflict with the constitution and laws of this State or of the United States; and to have and exercise all powers, and be subject to all duties usual and incident to trustees of corporations.

§ 2. The Superintendent of Public Instruction, by virtue of his office, shall be a member and secretary of said board, and shall report to the legislature at its regular sessions the condition and expenditures of said normal university, and communicate such further information as the said board of education or the legislature may direct.

§ 3. No member of the board of education shall receive any compensation for attendance on the meetings of the board, except his necessary traveling expenses; which shall be paid in the same manner as the instructors employed in the said normal university shall be paid. At all the stated and other meetings of the board, called by the president or secretary, or any five members of the board, five members shall constitute a quorum, provided all shall have been duly notified.

§ 4. The objects of the said normal nniversity shall be to qualify teachers for the common schools of this State, by imparting instruction in the art of teaching, and all branches of study which pertain to a common school education; in the elements of the natural sciences, including agricultural chemistry, animal and vegetable physiology; in the fundamental laws of the United States and the State of Illinois, in regard to the rights and duties of citizens, and such other studies as the board of education may, from time to time, prescribe.

§ 5. The board of education shall hold its first meeting at the office of the Superintendent of Public Instruction, on the first Tuesday in May next, at which meeting they shall appoint an agent, fixing his compensation, who shall visit the cities, villages and other places in the State, which may be deemed eligible for the purpose, to receive donations and proposals for the establishment and maintenance of the normal university. The board shall have power, and it shall be their duty, to fix the permanent location of said normal university, at the place where the most favorable inducements are offered for that purpose: *Provided,* that such location shall not be difficult of access, or detrimental to the welfare and prosperity of said normal university.

§ 6. The board of education shall appoint a principal, lecturer on scientific subjects, instructors and instructresses, together with such other officers as shall be required in the said normal university; fix their respective salaries and prescribe their several duties. They shall also have power to remove any of them for proper cause, after having given ten days' notice of any charge, which may be duly presented, and reasonable opportunity for defense. They shall also prescribe the text books, apparatus and furniture to be used in the university, and provide the same; and shall make all regulations necessary for its management. And the board shall have power to recognize auxiliary institutions when deemed practicable: *Provided,* that such auxiliary institutions shall not receive any appropriation from the treasury, or the seminary or university fund.

§ 7. Each county in the State shall be entitled to gratuitous instruction for *one pupil in said normal university; and

---

* Made two by act approved February 14, 1861.

each representative district shall be entitled to gratuitous instruction for a number of pupils equal to the number of representatives in said district, to be chosen in the following manner: The school commissioner [county superintendent] in each county shall receive and register the names of all applicants for admission in said normal university, and shall present the same to the county court, or, in counties acting under township organization, to the board of supervisors, which said county court or board of supervisors, as the case may be, shall, together with the county commissioner, examine all applicants so presented, in such a manner as the board of education may direct, and from the number of such as shall be found to possess the requisite qualifications, such pupils shall be selected by lot; and in representative districts composed of more than one county, the school commissioner and the county judge, or the school commissioner and chairman of the board of supervisors, in counties acting under township organization, as the case may be, of the several counties composing such representative district, shall meet at the clerk's office of the county court of the oldest county, and from the applicants so presented to the county court, or board of supervisors, of the several counties represented, and found to possess the requisite qualifications, shall select by lot the number of pupils to which said district is entitled. The board of education shall have the discretionary power, if any candidate does not sign and file with the secretary of the board a declaration that he or she shall teach in the public schools within the State, in case that engagements can be secured by reasonable efforts, to require such candidate to provide for the payment of such fees for tuition as the board may prescribe.

§ 8. The interest of the university and seminary fund, or such part thereof as may be found necessary, shall be and is hereby appropriated for the maintenance of said normal university, and shall be paid on the order of the board of education from the treasury of the State; but in no case shall any part of the interest of said fund be applied to the purchase of sites, or for buildings for said university.

§ 9. The board shall have power to appropriate the one thousand dollars received from the Messrs. Merriam, of Springfield, Massachusetts, by the late Superintendent, to the purchase of apparatus for the use of the normal university, when established, and hereafter all gifts, grants and demises which may be made to the said normal university shall be applied in accordance with the wishes of the donors of the same.

§ 10. The board of corporators herein named, and their successors, shall each of them hold their office for the term of six years: *Provided*, that at the first meeting of said board, the said corporators shall determine by lot, so that one-third shall hold their office for two years, one-third for four years and one-third for six years. The Governor, by and with the advice and consent of the Senate, shall fill all vacancies which shall, at any time, occur in said board, by appointment of suitable persons to fill the same.

§ 11. At the first meeting of the board, and at each biennial meeting thereafter, it shall be the duty of said board to elect one of their number president, who shall serve until the next biennial meeting of the board, and until his successor is elected.

§ 12. At each biennial meeting, it shall be the duty of the board to appoint a treasurer, who shall not be a member of the board, and who shall give bond with such security as the board may direct, conditioned for the faithful discharge of the duties of his office.

§ 13. This act shall take effect on and after its passage, and be published and distributed as an appendix to the school law.

APPROVED February 18, 1857.

---

SOUTHERN ILLINOIS NORMAL UNIVERSITY, CARBONDALE.

AN ACT *to establish and maintain the Southern Illinois Normal University.*

SECTION 1. *Be it enacted by the People of the State of Illinois, represented in the General Assembly:* That a body politic and corporate is hereby created, by the name of the Southern Illinois Normal University, to have perpetual succession, with power to contract and be contracted with, to sue and be sued, to plead and be impleaded, to receive, by any legal mode of transfer or conveyance, property of any description, and to have, hold and enjoy the same, with the rents and profits thereof, and to sell and convey the same; also, to make and use a corporate seal with power to break or change the same, and to adopt by-laws, rules and regulations for the government of its members, officers, agents and employés: *Provided*, such by-laws shall not conflict with the Constitution of the United States or of this State.

§ 2. The objects of the said Southern Illinois Normal University shall be to qualify teachers for the common schools of this State by imparting instruction in the art of teaching in all branches of study which pertain to a common school education, in the elements of the natural sciences, including agricultural chemistry, animal and vegetable physiology, in the fundamental laws of the United States, and of the State of Illinois, in regard to the rights and duties of citizens, and such other studies as the board of education may, from time to time, prescribe.

§ 3. The powers of the said corporation shall be vested in, and its duties performed by, a board of trustees, not exceeding five in number, to be appointed as hereinafter provided.

§ 4. Upon the passage of this act, the Governor shall nominate and, by and with the advice of the Senate, appoint five citizens of the State as trustees of said institution, two of whom shall serve for two years, and three for four years, and until their successors are appointed and enter on duty, and successors in each class shall be appointed in like manner for four years: *Provided*, that in case of a vacancy by death or otherwise, the Governor shall appoint a successor for the remainder of the term vacated: *Provided*, that not more than two members of said board shall be residents of any one county.

§ 5. The said trustees shall hold their first meeting at Centralia, within one month after the passage of this act, at which meeting they shall elect one of their body as president and another as secretary; and cause a regular record to be made and kept of all their proceedings. The said board shall also, whenever his services shall be required, appoint a treasurer, not a member of the board, who shall give bonds to the People of the State of Illinois in double the amount of the largest sum likely to come into his hands, the penalty to be fixed by the board, conditioned for the faithful discharge of his duties as treasurer, with two or more securities; the treasurer may also be required to executed bonds from time to time as the board may direct.

§ 6. The treasurer shall keep an accurate account of all moneys received and paid out; the account for articles and supplies of every kind purchased shall be kept and reported, so as to show the kind, quantity and cost thereof.

§ 7. No member, officer, agent or employé of the board shall be a party to or interested in any contract for materials, supplies or services other than such as pertain to their positions and duties.

§ 8. Accounts of this institution shall be stated and settled annually with the Auditor of Public Accounts, or with such person or persons as may be designated by law for that purpose. And the trustees shall, ten days previous to each regular session of the General Assembly, submit to the Governor a report of all their actions and proceedings in the execution of their trust. with a statement of all accounts connected therewith, to be by the Governor laid before the General Assembly.

§ 9. The said board shall meet quarterly at such places or place as may be agreed on, and, until the buildings are completed, as much oftener as may be necessary; and thereafter the meetings shall be at the university.

§ 10. The trustees shall, as soon as practicable, advertise for proposals from localities desiring to secure the location of said normal university, and shall receive, for not less than three months from the date of their first advertisement, proposals for points situated as hereinafter mentioned, to donate lands, buildings, bonds, moneys. or other valuable consideration, to the State in aid of the foundation and support of said university; and shall, at a time previously fixed by advertisement, open and examine such proposals, and locate the institution at such point as shall, all things considered, offer the most advantageous conditions. The land shall be selected south of the railroad, or within six miles north of said road, passing from St. Louis to Terre Haute, known as the Alton and Terre Haute railroad, with a view of obtaining a good supply of water and other conveniences for the use of the institution.

§ 11. Upon the selection and securing of the land aforesaid, the trustees shall proceed to contract for the erection of buildings in which to furnish educational facilities for such number of students as hereinafter provided for, together with the outhouses required for use, also for the improvement of the land so as to make it available for the use of the institution. The buildings shall not be more than two · stories in height, and be constructed upon the most approved plan for use, shall front to the east, and shall be of sufficient capacity to accommodate not exceeding three hundred students, with the officers and necessary attendants. The outside walls to be of hewn stone or brick, partition walls of brick, roofs of slate, and the whole buildings made fire-proof, and so constructed as to be warmed in the most healthy and economical manner, with ample ventilation in all its parts. The out-houses shall be so placed and constructed as to avoid all danger to the main buildings from fire originating in any one of them. The board shall appoint an honest, competent superintendent of the buildings and improvements aforesaid, whose duty shall be to be always present during the progress of the work, and see that every stone, brick and piece of timber used is sound and properly placed, and whose right it shall be to require contractors and their employés to conform to his directions in executing their contracts; *Provided, however*, that said board of trustees may appoint any one of their number such superintendent: *And, provided, further,* that the buildings aforesaid may be erected and improvements made under the direction of the board and its superintendent, without letting the same to contractors.

§ 12. The said board of trustees shall appoint instructors and instructresses, together with such other officers as may be required in the said normal university; fix their respective salaries and prescribe their several duties. They shall also have power to remove any of them for proper cause after having given ten days' notice of any charge which may be duly presented, and reasonable opportunity of defense. They shall also prescribe the text books, apparatus and furniture to be used in the university and provide the same, and shall make all regulations necessary for its management.

§ 13. All the counties shall be entitled to gratuitous instruction for two pupils for each county in said normal university, and each representative district shall be entitled to gratuitous in-

struction for a number of pupils equal to the number of representatives in said district, to be chosen in the following manner:
The superintendent of schools in each county shall receive and
register the names of all applicants for admission in said normal university, and shall present the same to the county court,
or, in counties acting under township organization, to the board
of supervisors, which said county court or board of supervisors, as the case may be, shall, together with the superintendent of schools, examine all applicants so presented, in such
manner as the board of trustees may direct; and from the number of such as shall be found to possess the requisite qualifications, such pupils shall be selected by lot, and in representative districts composed of more than one county, the superintendent of schools and county judge, or the superintendent of
schools and chairman of the board of supervisors in counties
acting under township organization, as the case may be, of the
several counties composing such representative district, shall
meet at the clerk's office of the county court of the oldest
county, and from the applicants so presented to the county
court or board of supervisors of the several counties represented, and found to possess the requisite qualifications, shall
select by lot the number of pupils to which said district is entitled.   The board of trustees shall have discretionary power,
if any candidate does not sign and file with the secretary of
the board a declaration that he or she will teach in the public
schools within the State not less than three years, in case that
engagements can be secured by reasonable efforts, to require
[the] candidate to provide for the payment of such fees for
tuition as the board may prescribe.

§ 14.   To enable the board of trustees to erect the buildings
and make the improvements preparatory to the reception of
pupils in said institution, and to supply the necessary furniture for the same, the sum of seventy-five thousand dollars is
hereby appropriated out of the State Treasury, payable on the
orders of said board, as required for use, in sums not exceeding ten thousand dollars per month.   The first payment to be
made on the first day of June next, and subsequent payments
monthly thereafter, but each successive order for subsequent
payments shall be accompanied by an account sustained by
vouchers, showing, to the satisfaction of the Auditor, the expenditure of the previous payment.

§ 15.   The expense of building, improving, repairing and
supplying fuel and furniture, and the salaries or compensation
of the trustees, superintendent, assistants, agents and employés,
shall be a charge upon the State Treasury; all other expenses
shall be chargeable against pupils, and the trustees shall regulate the charges accordingly.

§ 16.   If the buildings and improvements herein provided for
shall be ready for the reception of pupils before the next regular session of the General Assembly, the Governor is authorized to make orders on the Auditor, directing him to issue war-

rants at the end of each quarter of the fiscal year for amounts sufficient to pay the expenses chargeable against the State, and the Auditor shall issue warrants accordingly, which shall be paid by the Treasurer.

§ 17. Trustees of this institution shall receive their personal and traveling expenses, and the Auditor is hereby authorized to issue his warrants quarterly, upon taking the affidavit of the trustees as to the actual time employed, and their personal and traveling expenses.

§ 18. This act shall take effect and be in force from and after its passage.

APPROVED March 9, 1869.

EASTERN ILLINOIS STATE NORMAL SCHOOL, CHARLESTON.

AN [ACT] *to establish and maintain the Eastern Illinois State Normal School.*

SECTION 1. *Be it enacted by the People of the State of Illinois, represented in the General Assembly:* That a body politic and corporate is hereby created, by the name of the Eastern Illinois State Normal School, to have perpetual succession, with power to contract and be contracted with, to sue and be sued, to plead and be impleaded, to receive by any legal mode or transfer or conveyance property of any description, and to have and hold and enjoy the same; also to make and use a corporate seal with power to break or change the same, and adopt by-laws, rules and regulations for the government of its members, official agents and employés: *Provided,* such by-laws shall not conflict with the Constitution of the United States or of this State.

§ 2. The object of the said Eastern Illinois State Normal School shall be to qualify teachers for the common schools of this State by imparting instructions in the art of teaching in all branches of study which pertain to a common school education; in the elements of the natural and of the physical sciences; in the fundamental laws of the United States and of the State of Illinois, in regard to the rights and duties of citizens.

§ 3. The powers of the said corporation shall be vested [in], and its duties performed by, a board of trustees, not exceeding five in number, to be appointed as hereinafter provided.

§ 4. Upon the passage of this act, the Governor shall nominate, and, by and with the advice of the Senate, appoint five citizens who shall be residents of the State outside of the territory within which this school is to be located, as trustees of said institution, two of whom shall serve for two years and three for four years, and until their successors are appointed and enter on duty; and suecessors in each class shall be appointed in like manner for four years: *Provided*, that in case of a vacancy by death or otherwise, the Governor shall appoint a successor for the remainder of the term vacated: *Provided*, that no two members of said board shall be residents of any one county or in one senatorial district. The Superintendent of Public Instruction shall be a trustee of said school, ex-officio.

§ 5. The said trustees shall hold their first meeting at .... within one month from the time this act goes into effect, at which meeting they shall elect one of their body as president and another as secretary, and cause a regular record to be made and kept of all their proceedings. The said board shall also, whenever his services shall be required, appoint a treasurer, not a member of the board, who shall give bonds to the People of the State of Illinois in double the amount of the largest sum likely to come into his hands, the penalty to be fixed by the board, conditioned for the faithful discharge of his duties as treasurer, with two or more securities; the treasurer may also be required to execute bonds from time to time as the board may direct.

§ 6. The treasurer shall keep an accurate account of all moneys received and paid out; the account for articles and supplies of every kind purchased shall be kept and reported, so as to show the kind, quantity and cost thereof.

§ 7. No member, officer, agent or employé of the board shall be a party to, or interested in, any contract for materials or supplies.

§ 8. Accounts of this institution shall be stated and settled annually with the Auditor of Public Accounts, or with such person or persons as may be designated by law for that purpose. And the trustees shall, ten days previous to each regular session of the General Assembly, submit to the Governor a report of all their actions and proceedings in the execution of their trust, with a statement of all accounts connected therewith, to be by the Governor laid before the General Assembly.

§ 9. The said board shall meet quarterly at such place or places as may be agreed on, and, until the buildings are completed, as much oftener as may be necessary, and thereafter the meetings shall be at the school.

§ 10. The trustees shall, as soon as practicable after their appointment, arrange to receive from the localities desiring to secure the location of said school, proposals for donation of a site, of not less than forty acres of ground, and other valuable considerations, and shall locate the same in the place offering the most advantageous conditions, all things considered, in that portion of the State lying north of the Baltimore & Ohio Southwestern Railroad, and south of the Wabash Railroad, and east of the main line of the Illinois Central Railroad, and the

—8

counties through which said roads run, with a view of obtaining a good water supply and other conveniences for the use of the institution.

§ 11. Upon the selection and securing of the land aforesaid, the trustees shall proceed to secure plans, and to contract for the erection of buildings in which to furnish educational facilities for such number of students as hereinafter provided for, together with the out-houses required for use; also for the improvement of the land so as to make it available for the use of the institution. The buildings shall not be more than two stories in height, and be constructed upon the most approved plans for use, and shall be of sufficient capacity to accommodate not less than one thousand students, with the officers and necessary attendants. The outside walls to be of hewn stone or brick, partition walls of brick, or equally good fire-proof material; roof of slate, and the whole buildings made fire resisting, and so constructed as to be warmed in the most healthful and economical manner, with ample ventilation in all its parts. The out-houses shall be so placed and constructed as to avoid all danger to the main buildings from fire originating in any one of them. The board shall appoint a trustworthy and competent superintendent of the buildings and improvements aforesaid, whose duty it shall be to be always present during the progress of the work, and see that every brick, stone and piece of timber used is sound and properly placed, and whose right it shall be to require contractors and their employés to conform to his directions in executing their contracts: *Provided, however*, that said board of trustees shall not appoint any one of their number such superintendent: *And, provided, further*, that the buildings aforesaid may be erected and improvements made under the direction of the board and superintendent, without letting the same to contractors.

§ 12. The said board of trustees shall appoint instructors, together with such other officers as may be required in the said normal schools, fix their respective salaries and prescribe their several duties. They shall also have power to remove any of them for proper cause after having given ten days' notice of any charge which may be duly presented, and reasonable opportunity of defense. They shall also prescribe the text-books, apparatus and furniture to be used in the school, and provide the same, and shall make all regulations necessary for this management.

§ 13. All the counties of the State shall be entitled to gratuitous instruction for two pupils for each county in said normal school, and each representative district shall be entitled to gratuitous instruction for a number of pupils equal to the number of representatives in said district, to be chosen in the following manner: The superintendent of schools in each county shall receive and register the names of all applicants for admission in said normal school, and shall present the same to the county court, or in counties acting under township organization, to the board of supervisors, as the case may be, shall, together

with the superintendent of schools, examine all applicants so presented, in such manner as the board of trustees may direct; and
from the number of such as shall be found to possess the requisite
qualifications, such pupils shall be selected by lot; and in
representative districts composed of more than one county, the
superintendent of schools and county judge, or the superintendent of schools and the chairman of the board of supervisors in
counties acting under township organization, as the case may be,
of the several counties composing such representative district,
shall meet at the clerk's office of the county court of the oldest
county, and from the applicants so presented to the county court
or board of supervisors of the several counties represented, and
found to possess the requisite qualifications, shall select by lot
the pupils to which said district is entitled. The board of trustees shall have discretionary power, if any candidate does not
sign and file with the secretary of the board a declaration that he
or she will teach in the public schools within the State not less
than three years, in case that engagements can be secured by
reasonable efforts, to require the candidate to provide for the payment of such fees for tuition, as the board may prescribe.

§ 14. To enable the board of trustees to erect the buildings and make the improvements preparatory to the reception
of pupils in said institution, to supply the necessary furniture
for the same, and for the first year's instruction, the sum
of fifty thousand dollars is hereby appropriated out of the
State Treasury, payable on the orders of said board, as required for use, in sums not exceeding ten thousand dollars per
month; the first payment to be made on the first day of July,
1896, and subsequent payments shall be accompanied by an account, sustained by vouchers, showing to the satisfaction of the
Auditor and with the approval of the Governor, the expenditure
of the previous payment.

§ 15. The expense of the building, improving, repairing
and supplying fuel and furniture, and the necessary appliances
and apparatus for conducting said school, and the salaries or
compensation of trustees, superintendent, assistants, agents
and employés, shall be a charge upon the State Treasury;
all other expenses shall be chargeable against pupils and the
trustees shall regulate the charges accordingly.

§ 16. If the buildings and improvements herein provided
for shall be ready for the reception of pupils before the next
regular session of the the General Assembly, the Governor is
authorized to make orders on the Auditor, directing him to
issue warrants at the end of each quarter of the fiscal year
for amounts sufficient to pay expenses chargeable against the
State out of the above named appropriation of fifty thousand
dollars, and the Auditor shall issue warrants accordingly, which
shall be paid by the Treasurer.

§ 17. The trustees of the institution shall receive their personal and traveling expenses, and the Auditor is hereby author-

ized to issue warrants quarterly, upon taking the affidavit of the trustees as to the actual time employed, and their personal and traveling expenses.

APPROVED May 22, 1895.

---

NORTHERN ILLINOIS STATE NORMAL SCHOOL, DEKALB.

AN ACT *to establish and to maintain the Northern Illinois State Normal School.*

SECTION 1. *Be it enacted by the People of the State of Illinois, represented in the General Assembly:* That a body politic and corporate is hereby created, by the name of the Northern Illinois State Normal School, to have perpetual succession, with power to contract and be contracted with, to sue and be sued, to plead and be impleaded, to receive by any legal mode or transfer or conveyance property of any description, and to have and hold and enjoy the same; also to make and use a corporate seal with power to break or change the same, and adopt by-laws, rules and regulations for the government of its members, official agents and employés: *Provided*, such by-laws shall not conflict with the Constitution of the United States or of this State.

§ 2. The object of the said Northern Illinois State Normal School shall be to qualify teachers for the common schools of this State by imparting instruction in the art of teaching in all branches of study which pertain to a common school education, in the elements of the natural and of the physical sciences, in the fundamental laws of the United States and of the State of Illinois, in regard to the rights and duties of citizens.

§ 3. The powers of the said corporation shall be vested in, and its duties performed by, a board of trustees, not exceeding five in number, to be appointed as hereinafter provided.

§ 4. Upon the passage of this act, the Governor shall nominate, and by and with the advice of the Senate, appoint five citizens of the State as trustees of said institution, two of whom shall serve for two years, and three for four years, and until their successors are appointed and enter on duty, and successors in each class shall be appointed in like manner for four years: *Provided*, that in case of a vacancy by death or otherwise, the Governor shall appoint a successor for the remainder of the term vacated: *Provided*, that no two members of said board shall be residents of any one county, or in one congressional district. The Superintendent of Public Instruction shall be a trustee of this school, ex-officio.

§ 5. The said trustees shall hold their first meeting at ........within one month from the time this act goes into effect, at which meeting they shall elect one of their body as president and another as secretary, and cause a regular record to be made and kept of all their proceedings. The said board shall also, whenever his services shall be required, appoint a treasurer, not a member of the board, who shall give bonds to the People of the State of Illinois in double the amount of the largest sum likely to come into his hands, the penalty to be fixed by the board, conditioned for the faithful discharge of his duties as treasurer. with two or more securities; the treasurer may also be required to execute bonds from time to time as the board may direct.

§ 6. The treasurer shall keep an accurate account of all moneys received and paid out: the account for articles and supplies of every kind purchased shall be kept and reported, so as to show the kind, quantity and cost thereof.

§ 7. No member. officer, agen t or employé of the board shall be a party to or interested in any contract for materials or supplies.

§ 8. Accounts of this institution shall be stated and settled annually with the Auditor of Public Accounts, or with such person or persons as may be designated by law for that purpose. And the trustees shall, ten days previous to each regular session of the General Assembly, submit to the Governor a report of all their actions and proceedings in the execution of their trust, with a statement of all accounts connected therewith, to be by the Governor laid before the General Assembly.

§ 9. The said board shall meet quarterly at such place or places as may be agreed on. and, until the buildings are completed. as much oftener as may be necessary, and thereafter the meetings shall be at the school.

§ 10. The trustees, shall, as soon as practicable after their appointment, arrange to receive from the localities desiring to secure the location of said school, proposals for the donation of a site, of not less than forty acres of ground, and other valuable considerations, and shall locate the same in the place offering the most advantageous conditions, all things considered, as nearly central as possible in that portion of the State, lying north of the main line of the C., R. I. & P. R. R., with a view of obtaining a good water supply and other conveniences for the use of the institution.

§ 11. Upon the selection and securing the land aforesaid, the trustees shall proceed to secure plans and to contract for the erection of buildings in which to furnish educational facilities for such number of students as hereinafter provided for, together with the outhouses required for use, also for the improvement of the land so as to make it available for the use of the institution. The building shall not be more than two stories in height. and be constructed upon the most approved plan for use, and shall be of sufficient capacity to accommodate not less than one thousand students, with the officers and necessary attendants. The outside walls to be of hewn stone or brick, partition walls of brick, or equally good fire-proof material; roof of slate, and the whole buildings made fire-resisting, and so constructed as to be warmed in the most healthful and economical manner, with ample ventilation in all its parts. The out-houses shall be so placed and constructed as to avoid all danger to the main buildings from fire originating in any one of them. The board shall appoint a trustworthy and competent superintendent of the buildings and improvements aforesaid, whose duty it shall be to be always present during the progress of the work, and see that every brick, stone and piece of timber used is sound and properly placed, and whose right it shall be to require contractors and their employés to conform to his directions in executing their contracts: *Provided, however,* that said board of trustees shall not appoint any one of their number such superintendent: *And, provided, further,* that the buildings aforesaid may be erected and improvements made under the the direction of the board and superintendent, without letting the same to contractors.

§ 12. The said board of trustees shall appoint instructors, together with such other officers as may be required in the said normal schools, fix their respective salaries and prescribe their several duties. They shall also have power to remove any of them for proper cause after having given ten days notice of any charge which may be duly presented, and reasonable opportunity of defense. They shall also prescribe the text-books, apparatus and furniture to be used in the school and provide the same, and shall make all regulations necessary for this management.

§ 13. All the counties of the State shall be entitled to gratuitous instruction for two pupils for each county in said normal school, and each representative district shall be entitled to gratuitous instruction for a number of pupils equal to the number of representatives in said district, to be chosen in the following manner: The superintendent of schools in each county shall receive and register the names of all applicants for admission in said normal school and shall present the same to the county court, or in counties acting under township organization, to the board of supervisors, as the case may be, shall, together with the superintendent of schools, examine all applicants so presented, in such manner as the board of trustees may direct, and from the number of such as shall be found to possess the requisite qualifications, such pupils shall be selected by lot, and in representative districts composed of more than one county, the superintendent of schools and county judge, or the superintendent of schools and the chairman of the board of supervisors in the counties acting under township organization, as the case may be, of the several counties composing such representative district, shall meet at the clerk's office of the county court of the oldest county, and from the applicants so presented to the county court or board of supervisors of the several counties represented, and found to possess the requisite qualifications, shall select by lot the pupils to which said district is entitled. The board of trustees shall have discretionary power, if any candidate does not sign and file with the the secretary of the board a declaration that he or she will teach in the public schools within the State not less than three years, in case that engagements can be secured by reasonable efforts, to require the candidate to provide for the payment of such fees for tuition as the board may prescribe.

§ 14. To enable the board of trustees to erect the buildings and make the improvement preparatory to the reception of pupils in said institution, to supply the necessary furniture for the same, and for the first year's instruction, the sum of fifty thousand dollars is hereby appropriated out of the State Treasury, payable on the orders of said board, as required for use, in sums not exceeding ten thousand dollars per month, the first payment to be made on the first day of July, 1896, and subsequent payments shall be accompanied by an account, sustained by vouchers, showing to the satisfaction of the Auditor the expenditure of the previous payment, and approved by the Governor.

§ 15. The expense of the building, improving, repairing and supplying fuel and furniture, and the necessary appliances and apparatus for conducting said school, and the salaries or compensation of the trustees, superintendent, assistants, agents and employés, shall be a charge upon the State Treasury; all other expenses shall be chargeable against pupils, and the trustees shall regulate the charges accordingly.

§ 16. If the buildings and improvements herein provided for shall be ready for the reception of pupils before the next regular session of the General Assembly, the Governor is authorized to make orders on the Auditor, directing him to issue warrants at the end of each quarter of the fiscal year for amounts sufficient to pay expenses chargeable against the State out of the above named appropriation of fifty thousand dollars, and the Auditor shall issue warrants accordingly, which shall be paid by the Treasurer.

§ 17. The trustees of this institution shall receive their personal and traveling expenses, and the Auditor is hereby authorized to issue warrants quarterly, upon taking the affidavit of the trustees as to the actual time employed, and their personal and traveling expenses.

APPROVED May 22, 1895.

---

## COUNTY NORMAL SCHOOLS.

AN ACT *to enable counties to establish county normal schools.*

SECTION 1. *Be it enacted by the People of the State of Illinois, represented in the General Assembly:* That in each county adopting township organization, the board of supervisors, and in other counties the county court, may establish a county normal school for the purpose of fitting teachers for the common schools. That they shall be authorized to levy taxes and appropriate moneys for the support of said schools, and also for the purchase of necessary grounds and buildings, furniture, apparatus, etc., and to hold and acquire, by gift or purchase, either from individuals or corporations, any real estate, buildings or other property, for the use of said schools, said taxes to be levied and collected as all other county taxes: *Provided*, that in counties not under township organization, county courts shall not be authorized to proceed under the provisions of this act until the subject shall have been submitted to a vote of the people, at a general election, and it shall appear that a majority of all the votes cast on the subject, at said election, shall be in favor of the establishment of a county normal school. The ballots used in voting on this subject may read "For a county normal school," or "Against a county normal school."

§ 2. The management and control of said school shall be in a county board of education, consisting of not less than five or more than eight persons, of which board the chairman of the board of supervisors or the judge of the county court, as the case may be, and the county superintendent of schools, shall be *ex officio* members. The other members shall be chosen by the board of supervisors or county court, and shall hold their offices for the term of three years. But at the first election one-third shall be chosen for one year, one-third for two years. and one-third for three years, and thereafter one third shall be elected annually. Said election shall be held at the annual meeting of the board of supervisors in September, or at the September term of the county court, as the case may be.

§ 3. Said board of education shall have power to hire teachers, and to make and enforce all needful rules and regulations for the management of said schools. A majority of said board shall constitute a quorum for the transaction of business, and a meeting of said board may be called at any time by the president or secretary, or by any three of the members thereof. Said board shall proceed to organize, within twenty days after their appointment, by electing a president, who shall hold his office for one year, and until his successor shall be appointed. The county superintendent shall be, *ex officio*, secretary of the board. Said board shall make to the board of supervisors, at their annual meeting in September, or to the county court at the September term, as the case may be, a full report of the condition and expenditures of said county normal school, together with an estimate of the expenses of said school for the ensuing year.

§ 4. Two or more counties may unite in establishing a normal school, in which case the per cent. of tax levied for the support of said school shall be the same in each county.

§ 5. In all counties that have already established normal schools, the action of the board of supervisors in so doing, and all appropriations made by them for their support, are hereby legalized, and said board of supervisors are hereby authorized and empowered to make further appropriations for the support of such schools already established, until such schools shall have been established under the previous sections of this act.

§ 6. No member of the aforesaid county board of education shall be entitled to compensation for services rendered as a member of such board.

§ 7. This act shall be in force from and after its passage.
APPROVED March 15, 1869.

---

### THE ILLINOIS UNIVERSITY.

AN ACT *to provide for State scholarships in the University of Illinois, and the manner of awarding the same. Approved June 24, 1895. In force July 1, 1895.*

SECTION 1. *Be it enacted by the People of the State of Illinois, represented in the General Assembly:* That to equalize the advantages of the University of Illinois to all parts of the State, there shall be awarded annually, as hereinafter provided, to each county of the State one State scholarship, which shall entitle the holder thereof, who shall be a resident of the senatorial district to which he is accredited, to instruction in any or all departments of said University of Illinois for a term of four years, free from any charge for tuition or any incidental charge, unless such incidental charges shall have been made for materials used or for damages needlessly done to property of the University: *Provided*, that in counties having two or more senatorial districts, there shall be awarded annually one additional scholarship for each of said senatorial districts.

§ 2. A competitive examination under the direction of the Superintendent of Public Instruction shall be held at the county court house in each county of the State upon the first Saturday of June in each and every year by the county superintendent of schools, upon such branches of study as said Superintendent of Public Instruction and the President of said University may deem best.

§ 3. Questions for such examinations shall be prepared and furnished by the President of the University to the Superintendent of Public Instruction, who shall attend to the printing and distribution thereof to the several county superintendents of schools prior to such examinations.

§ 4. In case any candidate who shall be awarded a scholarship shall fail to pass the entrance examination to the University, or shall fail to claim the privileges of such scholarship, or, having claimed the privileges, shall be expelled, or for any reason shall abandon his right to, or vacate, such scholarship, either before or after entering thereupon, then the candidate certified to be next entitled in the same county shall become entitled to the same. In case any scholarship belonging to any county shall not be claimed by any candidate resident in that county, the Superintendent of Public Instruction may fill the same by appointing some candidate first entitled to a vacancy in some other county, after notice has been served upon the county superintendent of said first mentioned county.

§ 5. The county superintendents shall, within ten days after such examination, make and file in the office of the Superintendent of Public Instruction certificates, in which they shall name all the candidates examined, and specify the order of their excellence; and such candidates shall, in the order of their excellence, become entitled to the scholarships belonging to their respective counties. The examination papers handed in by each candidate shall also be filed with the certificate of examination.

§ 6. Candidates, to be eligible to said scholarship, shall be at least sixteen years of age, and shall have been *bona fide* residents of their respective counties for at least one year immediately preceding the examination.

§ 7. Any student holding a State scholarship, and who shall make it appear to the satisfaction of the President of the University that he requires leave of absence for the purpose of earning funds to defray his expenses while in attendance, may, in the discretion of the President, be granted such a leave of absence, and may be allowed a period not exceeding six years from commencement thereof for the completion of his course at said University.

§ 8. Notices of the time and place of the examination shall be given in the schools having pupils eligible thereto prior to the first day of January in each year. The Superintendent of Public Instruction shall attend to the giving of the notices hereinbefore provided for. He may, in his discretion, direct that the examination in any county may be held at some other time and place than that hereinbefore specified. He shall keep full records in his department of the reports of the different examiners, showing the age, post-office address and standing of each candidate, and shall notify candidates of their rights under this act. He is hereby charged with the general supervision and direction of all matters in connection with the filling of such scholarships. He shall determine any controversy which may arise under this act.

§ 9. Students enjoying the privileges of State scholarships shall, in common with other students of said University, be subject to all the examinations, rules and requirements of the board of trustees and faculty, except as herein provided.

§ 10. Nothing herein contained shall be construed to prevent the board of trustees of said University from granting such other free scholarships as in their discretion may be deemed best

123

# INDEX.

**PAGE.**

Accounts of county superintendent, how
 kept........................................ 11
 of township treasurer, examined by
 county superintendent................. 10
 same, how kept.......................... 33
 same, subject to inspection............ 84
 of township treasurer with school districts.................................... 37
 same, semi-annual statement of......... 37
Actions, civil--
 against collector of taxes............11, 64
 against county board................... 70
 against persons failing to pay over
 fines and forfeitures................. 81
 against purchaser of school lands...... 77
 against school officers...............83, 84
 against township treasurer... .. ...34, 83
 against township trustees ... 13, 18, 30, 83, 84
 against trespassers on school lands ... 75
 to recover interest ..................... 36
 to recover on mortgages................ 36
 to recover on notes, etc., belonging to
 the school fund.....................34, 36
Actions, criminal--
 against school officers................. 84
 against persons preventing colored
 children from attending school...... 86
 against trespassers on school lands ... 75
Acts, official, to be recorded ......... 19, 42, 51
 repealed................................ 88
 special, may be relinquished.......... 81
Administrators to give preference to debts
 due the school fund ................... 36
Advertisements of sale of school houses or
 site.................................... 21
 of sale of school lands....'.......... 22, 76
Advice given to school officers by State
 Superintendent........................ 5
 to school officers and teachers by county superintendents.................... 10
Age of persons enumerated in school census.................................... 20
 in statistics of illiteracy............ 20
 of school children..................... 43
 taken as basis of apportionment of
 funds .............................. 18, 19, 71
Apparatus, school may be purchased .... 45
 may not be sold by school teacher or
 officer ......................... 7, 43, 85
Appeal from county superintendent to
 State Superintendent................. 14
 from trustees to county superintendent ............................... 26, 27
Apportionment of funds by Auditor....... 71
 by county superintendent............. 18
 by township trustees.................. 19
Appraisal and distribution of district
 property, when a new district is
 formed. ... ...................29, 30
 of school lands........................ 76

**PAGE.**

Appraisers, how appointed................ 30
Assessor to note number of districts, in as-
 sessing personal property............ 63
Assistant of county superintendent....... 8
 his compensation...................... 9
Attachment, writ of, etc................. 34
Attorneys, State's, duties of, with regard
 to liens and forfeitures .... ....... 80
Auditor, State, to apportion public funds 71
 to withhold funds at request of State
 Superintendent...................... 6
 to file transcript of land sales....... 73
 to issue patents for school lands...... 73
 to issue warrant for pay of county
 superintendent...................9, 69
 when patents are lost to issue duplicates ............................. 79

Board of directors....................... 40
Board of Education of the State of Illinois, the...........................5, 99
Board of Education of the township—See
 "Township Board of Education."
Board of Education........................ 48
 appointed when......................52, 90
 elected when.........................48, 92
 funds withheld from................... 87
 in cities of 1,000, powers and duties of.. 50
 in cities of 100,000, powers and duties
 of..................................... 53
 in cities with special school charters... 92
 term of office of...................48, 90
 to make reports....................... 51
 to appoint a truant officer to enforce
 compulsory law....................... 96
Bond—
 official, county superintendent's....... 7
 approval of............................ 7
 custodian of........................... 8
 form of ............................. 7, 8
 insufficiency of....................... 8
 State Superintendent's, approval of.... 3
 custodian of........................... 3
 township treasurer's, approved by
 county superintendent............... 12
 same, by trustees..................... 32
 custodian of.......................... 12
 form of ............................. 33
 insufficiency of...................... 12
 same, trustees liable for ............. 84
Bonded debt, how disposed of in case of
 change of district lines............. 28
Bonds ................................... 64
 original issue of...................... 65
 same, amount limited.................. 65
 same, registry of..................... 65
 refunding without registration with
 Auditor............................. 66
 vote of people for the issue necessary... 65

Books. See "Text books".                    PAGE.
Boundaries, district.  See "District boun-
    daries "
Branches of study determined by direct-
    ors .........  :..................44,53,54,57
    by voters .......  ..  ...................  57
    See also "Teacher's certificate."

Census of children under 21 taken by
    county superintendent..............12, 13
    by directors..........................  42
    by trustees ..........................  20
    State basis of apportionment by Auditor 71
Certificate of amount of tax due each
    district...............................  62
    of tax levy ...  ........................  62
    how made when district lies in two
        or more counties .....................  62
Certificate of licensure, teachers...........54,56
    age of applicants ......................  57
    essential that the teacher have one
        good for the entire term of his con-
        tract.................  ........................44,57
    issued by county superintendents.......  56
    same, examinations for...................  56
    same, form of ...........................  57
    same, fee for. ...........................  57
    same, grades of .........................  56
    same, qualifications for..................  56
    same, record of.........................  57
    same, renewal of  ......................  57
    same, revocation of.....................  56
    issued by State Superintendent.........  56
    same, examination for..................  56
    same, revocation of......  .............  56
Certificate of purchase  See "Common
    school lands "
Changes of text books  ...................  44
Charitable institutions. State educational,
    visited by State Superintendent......  5
    to make report .  ..  ......  ...  6
Children, all to receive a good common
    school education......................1,43
    secured the right to instruction in the
        branches of an elementary educa-
        tion ...................................  96
    colored, rights of in public schools.....  86
    illiterate, number of reported.....  .....4,20
    number of in public schools, re-
        ported .....................4,20,42
    number of under 21, basis of appor-
        tionment....  ......  ......  13,19,71
    number of under 21, reported .......4,20,42
    penalty for employing, when under 13..  94
    penalty for failure to report ...........  84
    penalty for false report................  84
    under 13, unlawful to hire..............  94
Churches to receive no appropriation from
    school fund .............................  86
Cities and towns—
    of 1,000 inhabitants. ...................  49
    of 100,000 inhabitants .................  52
    to forfeit funds, when.................  87
    with special charters ...............51,52,87
    same, modified...  .  ...........61,87,90,91
Clerk of board of directors, appointed .....  43
    compensation of....  ..  .........  45
    to enter treasurer's exhibit on records..  36
    to keep a record  ....  ...............  43
    same, to submit to treasurer. ..........  42
    to post exhibit of treasurer at annual
        election ...:  .......................  44
    to report to township treasurer .......  43
    board of trustees.  See "Township
        treasurer."
Clerks of courts of record to report and pay
    over fines and forfeitures ............  80
Collectors of taxes— ,
    liability of, for non-payment of district
        taxes collected .......................  64

Collectors of taxes—                        PAGE.
    to give notice to directors and trus-
        tees ........  ...  ...  ............86,87
    to pay amount of Auditor's warrant to
        county superintendent...  .........  71
    to pay amount of district taxes col-
        lected to township treasurer  ........  63
    to state to township treasurer amount
        of district taxes uncollected......  ...  64
Colleges, etc., to report.  ..  ..........  87
Colored children in public schools..........  86
Common school lands--(16th section)..  ...  74
    business with regard thereto, where
        transacted .............................  74
    certificate of purchase of ...  ..........  78
    same, filed with county superintend-
        ent..  ....  ...........................78,79
    same, duplicate of..  .  ...............  79
    patents, conveying title to..............  78
    same, duplicates ...  ..................  79
    payment to secure purchase ............  77
    same, failure to make....................  77
    rental of.  ....  ........................  74
    right of way over, granted ............  75
    sale of.  ..  .  .....  ..................  75
    same, advertisement of................,.....76,77
    same, at private sale ...  ..  .............  78
    same, made by county superintendent..  78
    same, manner of ......................  78
    same, petition for......................  75
    same, in fractional townships..........  75
    same, notice of, given trustees .........  76
    same, place of .........................  77
    same, terms of ......................  77
    sale of at subsequent time ...........  78
    statement of sales of, to county board  78
    same, examined and recorded. ........  78
    same, transcript of, filed with Auditor..  78
    trustees to divide into lots and plat ...  76
    to value lots  ..........................  76
    to re-value lots  .........................  78
    See also "Real estate "
Compensation of school officers. ...  .......  88
    of assistants of county superintendent.  9
    of clerk of board of directors............  45
    of county superintendent..............  9
    of township treasurer...................  40
Compulsory attendance. .................  96
Condemnation of land for school site ......  46
Consolidation of districts.  See "District
    boundaries "
    of townships.  See "Township."
Constitution of Illinois, 1870, Art. V, Sec.
    1, and Art. VIII of .....  ...........  1
Contracts made by boards of trustees and
    directors, members not to be inter-
        ested in.....  ..  ....  ..........43,85
    made with teachers, conditions of va-
        lidity of. .........................55,56
Control of school houses .  ................  45
Controversies arising under school law.....  14
    appeal of, to State Superintendent ,.....  5
Conveyance of real estate by county super-
    intendent...........................11,79
    by trustees .........................  22,76
    to cities in trust..  .  .................  55
Corporation, board of education, a.........  49
    board of directors, a ..................  40
    board of trustees, a...................  15
    not to make sectarian grants....  .....1,85
Costs not chargeable to school officers,
    when .................................  86
County board.............................  69
    bills of county superintendent to be
        audited by  .......................9,70
    bond of county superintendent ap-
        proved by. ....  ...................  7
    examination of report of land sales by 9,70
    liability of, for failure to make examin-
        ation...............................70,71

County board--                                PAGE.
    may require new bond of county su-
      perintendent......................  .....   69
    must furnish office and supplies.......   70
    removal of county superintendent by
      vacancy in office of county superin-
      tendent..............................   70
County clerk...............................   67
    election of trustees, ordered by.......   16
    list of trustees furnished county super-
      intendent by.....................18,67
    map of township, filed by...............   27
    tax-payers, list of, filed by............27,67
    to compute district taxes....  ..........   68
    to certify to same to township treas-
      urers.................................   68
    to record statement of land sales......   69
    to transmit county superintendent's
      bill to State Auditor..................   69
County fund--
    consists of what........................   71
    loaned by county superintendent.......   14
County superintendent of schools....  ....    7
    accounts of township treasurer, exam-
      ined by..............................   10
    adviser of school teachers and officers..   10
    appeal from, to State Superintendent..   14
    appeal to, from action of trustees......   10
    apportionment of funds by.............   18
    same, of interest on county fund.......   13
    assistant of.............................    8
    bond of................................    7
    bond of township treasurer, approved
      and held by..........................   13
    may demand that same be increased...   32
    certificate, teacher's, may grant.......10,56
    same, may renew or revoke...........11,56
    same, to make record of...............10,57
    compensation of......................  8,9
    controversies under school law, referred
      to .....................................   14
    county funds, loaned by ...............   13
    directors, may order election of........   41
    same, may remove...................11,47
    election of............................    7
    examination of teachers, to make.....10,56
    examination of treasurer's accounts,
      etc , to make..........................   10
    fines and forfeitures, duties of, concern-
      ing...................................13,80
    funds, withheld by......................13,87
    may be chosen...........................    2
    notes, etc., taken by.....................   14
    oath of office, taken by..................    7
    office for ...............................    8
    office turned over to successor by ......   14
    qualifications of ........................    2
    real estate, may sell and convey, and
      lease ...   ........................11,79
    records, kept by..........................   11
    removal of, by county board...........   69
    report of, to county board ..........11,78
    same, to State Superintendent.........   12
    same, to trustees, on treasurer's ac-
      counts, etc............................   10
    sale of common school lands by. See
      "Common school lands."
    schools visited by.......................    9
    statistics of townships, may make up..   12
    same, cost of may collect from trus-
      tees....................................   18
    supplies for.............................    8
    teachers examined by......  .......10,56
    teachers' institutes conducted by....10,58
    treasurer's accounts examined by......   10
    treasurer's bonds approved and held
      by..........  ...........  ..........   13
    trustees, election of, ordered by........   10
    vacancy in office of, how filled........    8
County treasurer to give notice to directors
      and trustees ..........................   86

Debt, bonded, how disposed of in case of               PAGE.
    change of district lines ...............   28
Debts of old districts to be deducted......   30
    due school funds, preferred claims ......   36
    same, may be compromised by trus-
      tees....................................   22
Default in payment of loans or interest
      thereon...............................   36
    penalty for same .......................   36
Demands against school officers, lien for,
    upon real estate .......................   84
Diploma of county normal school some-
    times qualification for first grade
    certificate..............................   56
Directors of schools, a body politic and
    corporate...............................   40
    boards of, elected ......................   40
    apparatus purchased by, when..........   45
Directors of schools--
    bonds issued by......................46,64
    bonds refunded by......................   66
    branches of study prescribed by......44,54
    certificate of tax levy made by.........   62
    same, when to return...................   62
    same, when district is in two or more
      counties.  ...........................   62
    clerk of, see "Clerk."
    dismissal of teacher....................   45
    duties of, with regard to the schools..43,45
    election of..............................   40
    same, notices of .......................   41
    same, ordered by county superintend-
      ent....................................   41
    same, ordered by township treasurer...   41
    election of, on Saturday ................   41
    same, postponed.........................   41
    elections to choose school sites, etc,
      called by............................46,65
    exclusion of colored children from
      schools by, prohibited ...............   86
    exhibit by township treasurer to ......   37
    same, posted by, at annual election.....   38
    interest in contract made by the board,
      prohibited to .........................   43
    same, in sales of books, etc., used in
      the district, prohibited to........2,43,85
    interest on teachers' orders, to pay
      when ...............................38,61
    judges of district elections............   41
    judgments and executions against ....   88
    for conversion of school fund........   84
    for failure to discharge duties of
      office ........................88,84,85
    for failure to make returns, or for
      making false returns of statistics..   84
    for loss of school funds ...............   85
    for perversion of school funds to
      sectarian purposes..  ..............   85
    to district.............................   83
    liable.......................46,47,83,84,85
    libraries and apparatus purchased by,
      when .................................   45
    may assume indebtedness created for
      district.................................   95
    may borrow money, when.............   65
    may compensate clerk...  ...........   45
    may not be trustees ...................   40
    meeting of .............................   42
    names of teachers reported to county
      superintendent by ...................   43
    non-residence of members of, consti-
      tutes vacancy..........................   40
    official business of, how transacted.....   42
    orders drawn by...................44,46,47
    same, may not be drawn when ......44,46
    organization ...........................   42
    poll-book, returned by .................   42
    power of, to tax.......................61,62
    same, limitations..................62,64,65
    powers of, limited.......................   62

**Directors of schools—** PAGE.
president of board...................... 42
property of district, personal, sale of,
by........................................ 45
pupils transferred by .................. 47
same, amount due on account of, collected by ............................. 47
qualifications of ....................... 40
quorum of................................ 42
records kept by.......................... 42
records, submitted to treasurer........ 42
removal of .............................. 47
reports to treasurer .................... 42
schedules, certified by..................44,60
same, delivered to township treasurer
by........................................ 44
same, delivery of limited................ 44
same, receipted for...................... 60
schedules, separate, delivered by,
when ..............................47,59
school house controlled by............... 45
same, use of for meetings granted by... 45
school house site, located by, when..... 46
teachers, employment of, by............. 43
same, how limited .....................44,57
teachers, payment of, by................. 44
same, how limited........................ 44
term of office........................... 41
tie at election of ...................... 41
to notify collector of taxes to whom to
pay the money belonging to a union
district.....................43,64
transfer of pupils by.................... 47
truant officer appointed by....... ..... 96
vacancy in office of, how filled........ 41
women may be elected ................40,86
District, boundaries of, how changed .....25,52
township a, for high school...........23,24
Districting of newly organized township... 25
Districts, changes of ...................... 25
dissolved, when.......................... 30
divided by county lines, taxation in.... 62
elections in ....................28,42,48
elections to vote on change.............. 25
formation of ............................ 25
funds of, held by township treasurer.... 22
indebtedness created for, may be assumed................................... 95
list of taxpayers in, to be filed ....... 27
maps of, made and filed.................. 27
property of, held by trustees............ 21
same, when divided ...................... 30
taxes of. See "Taxes,"
with 1,000 inhabitants .................. 48
with 100,000 inhabitants................. 52
See "Union Districts."
Division of property of a district........ 30
Donations, etc., for school purposes........1,21,
same, for sectarian purposes, prohibited....................................1,85

Education, good common school, to be af-
forded all children....................... 1
elementary, secured to children......... 96
Effects of alcohol and narcotics............ 91
Elections. See "State Superintendent;"
"County Superintendent;" "Directors
of Schools;" "Township Trustees;"
"Boards of Education."
to purchase, move or build a school
house.................................... 46
Eligibility to office, to board of education ..................................... 58
to board of directors.................... 40
to board of trustees .................... 16
to township treasurership............... 19
Eligibility of women to office under school
laws..................................40,86
Enumeration of children. See "Census."
separate, made when..................... 20

Examination of books, accounts, etc., of
county superintendent by county
board.................................12,70
of directors by township treasurer..... 42
of treasurer by county superintendent .................................... 10
same, by trustees ....................... 21
Examination of teachers by county superintendent ...........................10,56
for State certificates ..................5,56
Execution issued against directors and
trustees................................. 86
Executors to give preference to school
debts................................... 36
Exemption from road labor and military
duty.................................... 88
Expulsion of pupils by directors .......... 45

False returns of children................. 84
Fines. See "Penalties."
Fines and forfeitures..................... 80
Flags on school houses..............102,103,104
Forfeiture of funds by townships......... 20
Form of bond of county superintendent... 7
of bond of township treasurer......... 33
of notice to districts affected by
changes proposed..................... 26
of mortgage ............................ 35
of orders by directors ................. 47
of register ............................ 59
of schedule and certificates thereto .... 60
of school orders......................47,73
of tax certificates..................... 62
of teacher's certificates and record.... 57
of treasurer's record of notes.......... 34
Fractional townships. See Townships
fractional."
Free schools established................... 1
Fund, school, county, consists of what.... 72
interest on, distributed..............13,72
principal of, loaned.................... 14
real estate belonging to .............. 79
Fund, school, State, consists of what...... 71
distributed ............................ 71
Funds, school, township, consist of
what ................................... 72
interest distributed.................... 72
principal loaned.....................34,72
real estate belonging to.............21,72
Funds. See "Apportionment of funds."
forfeiture of .......................... 20
withheld by county superintendent....13,87
same, by order of State Superintendent .................................... 6
Funds, school district, custodian of........ 22
how paid out ........................... 73
surplus loaned ......................... 35
union district's collected in one treasurer's hands .........................43,64
Furniture, school, sale of by school officers
prohibited ...........................2,85
purchase of............................. 62

General Assembly to establish free
schools................................. 1
Governor to approve State Superintendent's bond ............................. 3
Graduates of county normal schools....... 56

High school, township. See "Township
high school."
Holidays.................................. 61

Illinois State Normal University.......... 99
Illiteracy, report of ....................4,20
Imprisonment of school officers..........84,85

PAGE.
Indebtedness created for certain districts
  may be assumed by directors ....... 95
  previous, tax to pay, not limited....... 62
  refunded ...........................66,67
Indictment of school officers..............84,85
  of trespasser............................. 75
Informer to receive half.................... 75
Institutes, superintendents to assist in....10,58
  fees for .................................... 58
  teachers may attend without deduction
    of wages................................. 58
Institutions of learning to report.......... 87
Insurance of improvements on real estate
  loans................................... 86
Interest, action to recover................. 87
  added to principal.................87,72,73
  distributed.........................37,72
  on teacher's orders unpaid............. 61
  same, how stopped..................... 61
  penalty for default in payment of...... 36
  rates on bonds.......................65,67
  rates on loans........................... 34
  State to pay............................. 71

Judges of elections of directors............. 41
  delivery of poll-book by................. 42
Judges of elections of tru-tees............. 16
  delivery of poll-book by................. 18
Judgments against school officers........ 88
  against purchasers of school lands.. ... 77
Justices, duties of, concerning fines and forfeitures ................................. 80

Kindergarten schools ...................98,99

Lands  See "Common School Lands" and
  "Real Estate."
Levy of taxes  See "Taxes."
Liability of school officers................. 83
Libraries, school, provisions for.........45,50
Lien on real estate of school officers from
  date of issuing process................. 84
Limit of indebtedness, bonds, etc..........65,67
  of taxation........................62,65
Loans of county funds..................... 14
  of district funds, surplus............... 35
  of township fund....................34,35
Loss of funds, liability for................. 85

Mandamus, writ of........................ 88
Map of township......................... 39
  filed in twenty days by township treas-
    urer... .................................. 39
Meetings, of directors..................... 42
  of trustees............................. 19
  in school houses........................ 45
Miscellaneous............................. 86
Month, school............................. 61
Mortgages —
  form for................................. 35
  in name of county superintendent.....14,34
  in name of trustees..................22,34

Normal schools, county, act establishing... 119
  State, acts establishing.............105,119
Notes, etc., in name of county superintendent..................................... 14
  same, examined by county board ..... 70
  in name of trustees..................... 34
  same, examined by county superintend-
    ent..................................... 10
  by trustees............................. 21
  same, list of given county superintend-
    ent, annually........................... 35
Notice of elections, district..........29,41,49,65
  same, township..................16,17,23
  same, city, etc , to organize under gen-
    eral law, school...................52,98
  of examinations of teachers by county
    superintendent......................... 57

PAGE.
Notice of examination of teachers—
  by State Superintendent................. 56
  of sale of common school lands........ 76
  of sale of real estate.................... 21

Oath, official, county superintendent's...... 7
  State Superintendent's................. 3
Office of county superintendent............ 8
Office of State Superintendent, where kept.. 4
Office supplies............................. 8
Officers, school, exempt from road labor
  and military duty...................... 88
  liabilities of, See "Penalties."
  lien on real estate of................... 84
  to receive advice.....................4,10
Orders, school, form of...............47,73
  when against uncollected taxes........ 46
  teachers, substance of..............61,73
  same, draw interest, when............. 61
  same, to be drawn when............... 61
  treasurers to file....................... 73
Organization of board of directors......... 42
  of board of trustees.................... 19
  of cities, etc., under general law.......48,52

Parents must send children to school...... 96
Patents issued to purchasers of school
  lands.................................78,79
  same, duplicates of..................... 79
Penalties, who subject to—
  any person for preventing colored chil-
    dren from attending school.......... 86
  for trespass on school lands........... 75
  any school officer, for causing loss of
    school funds.......................... 85
  for neglect of duty.................5,84,85
  any school officer, or any other person
    for conversion or perversion of school
    funds..............................84,85
  borrower of school funds, for failure to
    pay interest or principal.............. 86
  cities, for failure to make report........ 87
  collectors of taxes, for refusal to pay..64,72
  county board, for neglect of duty to ex-
    amine report of land sales..........70,71
  clerks of courts of record, state's attor-
    neys and justices, for failure to report
    and to collect and pay over fines and
    forfeitures ........................80,81
  directors. See "Directors liable."
  parents, for keeping children from
    school .............................94,96
  parents, employers, etc., for the hiring
    of children under 13 years of age...... 94
  purchaser of school lands for not secur-
    ing payment........................... 77
  townships, for failure in delivering re-
    ports .................................. 20
  teachers, for not making schedules..... 58
  treasurers See "Treasurers liable."
  trustees. See "Trustees liable."
  See also, "Removal from office."
Permits to transfer pupils................. 47
  to be filed.............................. 47
Perversion of funds to sectarian uses...... 85
  penalty for............................. 85
Petition for change of district lines......... 25
  same, to be filed twenty days.......... 26
  same, notice of to districts............. 26
  for or against township high school.... 33
  for sale of school house ............... 21
  for organization under the general
    law ...............................52,98
  for purchase of school sites, etc........ 50
  for sale of school lands ............... 75
Plat of common school lands............. 76

128

Poll-book, election of directors, return of... 42
  same, penalty for failure............... 42
  election of trustees, return of........... 18
  same, penalty for failure............... 18
Polling places, more than one, when........ 17
Polls, election of directors, opened and
  closed.............................17,41
  election of trustees ................... 17
Poor children, books for................... 44
Postponement of election............17,41
President board of directors............ 42
  pro tempore, may be appointed........ 42
  of board of trustees............... 19
  pro tempore may be appointed........ 19
Proceedings, official, to be recorded......19,42
Property of districts, divided in case of
  change of district boundaries......... 29
  teachers to account for................ 58
Publication of statement by township
  treasurer.......................37,38,39
Pupils, age of ............................ 43
  age and name noted on register......58,59
  same, on schedule.... ...........59,60
  assigned to the several schools........ 45
  attendance of, noted.................59,60
  suspension and expulsion of........... 43
  transferred........................ 47
  same, separate schedules of, when...... 47
  under 12, in school four hours a day.... 45
Purchaser of common school lands........ 77
  may borrow amount of bid............ 77
  must secure payment of bid........... 77
  to receive certificates of purchase...... 79
  to receive patents.................. 78
  when to receive duplicates........... 79

Qualifications, for office county superintendent.............................. 2
  directors....... .................... 40
  treasurer........ ................... 19
  trustees............................ 16
  of teachers........................ 56
  of voters.......................... 17
  of women as school officers...........40,86
Quorum of directors.................... 42
  of trustees......................... 19

Rate of interest  See "Interest"
Real estate held by county superintendent..............................11,79
  by trustees........................ 22
  leased .......................11,22,74
  lien on, belonging to school officers..... 84
  released........................... 36
  right of way over, granted............ 79
  security for loans..................34,35
  same, how valued.................. 34
  taken for indebtedness by county superintendent........................11,75
  by trustees........................ 22
  See also "Common school lands."
Receipts for schedules............... 60
  treasurer to take and file............. 73
Records of county superintendents.....10,57,78
  same, examined by county board....12,78
  of directors........................ 42
  same, submitted to township treasurer. 42
  of sale of common school lands....... 78
  same, examined by county board...... 70
  same, transcript of, filed with Auditor.............................. 78
  of State Superintendent............. 4
  of teachers' certificates granted by
  county superintendent............. 57
  of treasurer.....................33,34
  same, examined by county superintendent.............................. 10
  same, open for inspection...........19,34

Records of county superintendents--
  same, submitted to trustees........... 37
  of trustees........................ 19
  same, open for inspection..........19,34
Registers, books furnished by directors..... 59
  same, returned by teachers at close of
  term............................ 59
  form of........................... 59
  to be kept by teachers..............58,59
Registration fee....................... 53
Relinquishment of special charter........ 52
Removal from district or township, effect
  of................................ 40
  from office--
  of county superintendent........... 69
  of directors....................... 47
  of president of board of trustees...... 19
  of teachers.....................45,51
  of treasurers..................... 19
Repeal of former acts .................. 88
Reports of cities and towns............. 87
  of collector of taxes to township treasurer............................63,64
  to trustees and directors ..........86,87
  of county superintendent to county
  board, annual.... .............. 12
  same, of land sales to county board...11,70
  same, to Auditor .................9,73
  same, of condition of schools to State
  Superintendent.................. 12
  of directors to township treasurer..... 42
  same, to county superintendent ...... 43
  same, to voters at annual meeting..... 43
  of fines and forfeitures ............. 80
  of institutions of learning............ 87
  of rentals to county superintendent.... 74
  of State Superintendent to Governor... 4
  of statistics. See "Statistics."
  of treasurer to trustees, annual and
  semi-annual...................... 37
  of trustees to county superintendent.... 19
  same, items of.................... 20
  penalties for failure to make. See "Penalties".......................... 84
Revenue and taxation................. 61
Rules and regulations made by board of
  education........................ 51
  by directors...................... 4
  by State Superintendent............ 5

Salary of State Superintendent.......... 3
Sale of common school lands. See "School
  lands."
  of real estate  See "Real estate."
  of school books, etc., limitations......2,85
  of school house and site............. 21
  of school property................. 45
Schedules, certificates upon, form........59,60
  delivery of to directors............. 60
  to township treasurer.............. 44
  form of.......................... 60
  receipt for, given to teacher......... 60
  teacher to keep................... 59
Scholars. See "Pupils"
School, any gift, etc., to..............1,21
School books. See "Text books."
School books, apparatus and furniture,
  school officers not to be interested in
  when..........................2,43,85
School directors. See "Directors."
School districts. See "Districts."
School elections. See "Elections."
School funds.......................... 71
School houses, building of, tax for limited........................... 61,62
  same, vote necessary to authorize..... 46
  controlled by directors............. 45
  meetings in....................... 45
  repairing and improving..........46,53,61
  site of........................... 46
  title to, in trustees................ 21

| | PAGE. |
|---|---|
School Inspectors..................97,98
School lands .....................74
School libraries..................45,62
School month......................61

School officers—
exempted from rond labor and military duty...................88
legal advisers of.............4,10
liable for conversion of school funds....84
for exclusion of colored children.......86
for failure to return, or false return of statistics...................84
for loss of school funds.............85
for perversion of same.............85
lien on real estate of .............84
selling school books, etc., by, prohibited when....................2,85
See also "Superintendent of Public Instruction and other officers."
School orders See "Orders."
School site. See "Site."
School Superintendent. See "Supt."
School tax. See "Taxes."
School trustees. See "Trustees of Schools"
School visitation.................9,43,50
School teachers. See "Teachers."
School year ......................43,44
Schools, branches of study in, how determined.......................44,50,57
high. See "Township high schools."
management of...............24,43,50,53
normal.......................99,102,106
supervision of....................4,9
support of .......................43,50
term, in cities..................50
same, in 'districts..............43,46
same, may be extended how.........46
visitation of...................9,43
Secretary of State to hold State Superintendent's bond ..............3
Sectarian purposes, perversion of funds to, prohibited ......................1,85
Security on bonds. See "Bonds, official."
personal, on loans...............84
real estate, on loans............84
same, improvements on, to be valued .86
Settlement, trustees may make.........22
Site, school house, choice of.......46,53
same, when made by directors.......46
sale of.........................21
condemnation of land for.........46,47
title held by trustees...........21
Sixteenth section, constitutes common school lands.................74
other sections in lieu of .........74
Southern Illinois Normal University....102
Special acts may be relinquished...51,52,93
modified in certain cases .......82,87,90
not repealed. .................87
State to pay interest............71
State's attorney. See "Attorneys."
State certificates................5,56
charitable institutions, superintendent of, to report ..............6
State charitable institutions, visited by State Superintendent..............5
State funds........................71
State normal schools............99,102
State Superintendent. See "Superintendent of Public Instruction."
Statements, made by teachers.........59
Statistics, not divisible, how reported...20,21
See "Reports."
Sufficiency of treasurer's securities, trustees responsible for .............84
Suits See "Actions."
Superintendent of Public Instruction ......3
adviser of county superintendents......4
bond of.........................3

| | PAGE. |
|---|---|
Superintendent of Public Instruction—
certificates, State teachers' granted and revoked by..................5,56
election of ....................3
forfeitures remitted by..........6
funds withheld by...............6
not to be interested in the sale of school books, etc...................2,85
oath of office of ...............3
office of, at seat of government....4
same, expense of.................3
papers, etc., filed and preserved by....4
record kept by...................4
report of, to the Governor.........4
rules to enforce the school law, made by.............................5
salary of, determined by law.......3
term of office of ...............3
to advise school officers.........5
to counsel and advise with teachers....4
to have supervision of the public schools.........................4
to visit State charitable institutions ...5
Superintendents of State charitable institutions to report to State Superintendent ..........................5
Superintendents of schools, appointed when............................50
Sureties See "Bonds, official."
Suspension of pupils................45

Taxes, school, collection of..........63
computation of, basis of..........62
same, made by county clerk ......62,63
collector of, to pay how, in case of union districts........................64
same, to pay township treasurer....63
same, failure to pay.............64
levy of, form of certificate.......62
same, when returned.............62
must be uniform.................63
power to levy, granted board of education in cities and villages.....50,61,62
to directors...................46,62
same, limited..................46,62
same, in satisfaction and judgment.....88
Taxpayers, list of filed...........28
Teachers, appointment of..........43,50,53
cannot be paid, when.........44,57,58,59
cannot be employed, when.........57
dismissal of..................45,51
examination of...............50,56,57
funds withheld from .............6
must have certificate.........44,57
names of, reported to county supt......43
not to teach on holidays..........61
pension fund ...............99,100,101
registers to be kept by .........58,59
same, returned to directors.......59
schedule to be kept by...........59
same, certified ................60
same, unpaid, balance of to draw interest...........................61
statements made by..............59
wages of, due when..............61
teachers, certificates of.........56
Teachers' Institutes held by county superintendent...................10,58
fees for .......................57
teachers may attend without deduction of wages.......................58
Term of office of boards of education.....23,49
of county superintendent.........7
of directors...................41
of State Superintendent.........3
of treasurer...................19
of trustees...................15
Terms of loaning school funds.........34
of sale of school lands..........77

—9 S

PAGE.

Text books prescribed by directors......... 44
 same, to be uniform..................... 44
 same, not to be changed oftener than
  once in four years........................ 44
 same, for poor children..... ........... 44
 same, not to be sold by school officers..2,85
Tie vote, how decided....................17,41
Title to real estate—
 to school houses and lots.............. 21
 to common school lands, from the
  State................................74,78
Town meeting, election of trustees at...... 18
Towns and cities. See "Cities and Towns.",

Township, school business of, done by trustees........................................ 15
 congressional, made a school township. 15
 divided by county lines................. 20
 same, tax in.............................. 62
 fractional, consolidated with adjacent,
  when..................................15,76
 fund of. See "Fund."
 funds apportioned to..................... 13
 same, forfeiture of....................6,20
 made a district to support a high
  school................................23,24
 may unite with another or with parts of
  oth.rs for the same purpose..........23, 24
 newly organized, districted............. 25
 same, map of............................. 25
 redistricted.............................. 52
 school section belonging to.............. 74

Township board of education.............. 23
 term of office............................ 23
 duties.................................... 24

Township high school, how discontinued... 24
 same, disposition of property........... 24
 how established........................... 23
 how supported............................ 24

Township treasurer..... ................... 32
 accounts of how kept..................... 33
 appointment of........................... 19
 same, who eligible to.................... 19
 bond official, approved...............18,32
 same, recorded........................... 13
 delivered to county superintendent....18,32
 form of................................... 33
 increased when............................ 32
 books and accounts of, examined by
  county superintendent.................. 10
 by trustees............................21,37
 same, subject to inspection...........19,31
 same, submitted to trustees............ 37
 certificate of amount of taxes due sent
  to, by county clerk................... 68
 certificate of tax levy returned by, to
  county clerk.......................... 38
 clerks of trustees, to be................ 19
 compensation of.......................... 40
 county superintendent may direct in
  case of change of district lines...... 27
 custodian, only legal, of funds of boards
  of education, when.................... 51
 of district funds......................... 22
 of township funds......................... 37
 debts due township probated by........ 36
 district funds paid out by, how........ 47
 district records examined by............. 38
 election of trustees, called by.......... 38
 duties of, as to transfer of pupils....38,47
 same, of directors....................... 47
 interest paid teachers by, when......... 38
 liable in a civil action—
  for failure or refusal to perform legal
   duties..............................39,88
  same, when not liable...............39,88
  for failure to publish annual statement 39
  for failure to turn over books, etc., to
   his successor........................ 83

PAGE.

Township treasurer—
 liable in a criminal action—
  for loss of school funds.............. 85
  for conversion of school funds .... .. 84
  for failure to report statistics, or for
   false return of same............ ....84,85
  for perversion of school funds to a sectarian use........................... 85
  for being interested in the sale of
   school books, etc....................2,85
  lien on real estate of................... 84
 list of taxpayers made and filed by..... 39
 maps made and filed by................... 39
 money paid to, by tax collector........ 63
 moneys, bonds, etc., delivered to, on
  certified statement of county superintendent............................... 13
 not to be interested in the sale of school
  books, etc., when.....................2,85
 notes, bonds, etc., held by, examined by
  county superintendent................. 10
 same, list of, given to county superintendent annually....................... 35
 same, submitted to trustees............. 37
 cash held by, verified by trustees....... 37
 official term of, two years.............. 19
 poll-book of district election filed with. 42
 removed by trustees, when.............. 22
 responsible for losses, when............. 85
 State and county funds paid to, by
  county superintendent................. 13
 Statement to directors, made by under
  oath semi-annually................37,38
 statement to trustees................... 37
 sued by trustees, when.................. 22
 suit brought by, against tax-collector.. 64
 same, to recover interest............... 36
 same, when additional security is not
  given................................. 34
 surplus of district funds, loaned by..... 35
 to make teachers' orders interest bear-
  ing when not paid on presentation ..38,61
 same, to record.......................... 38
 to file orders paid...................... 73
 to notify clerks of directors when he
  has funds to pay unpaid teachers' orders..................................38,61
 same, to record.......................... 38
 to hold funds to pay same...... ....... 38
 to take and file receipts for money paid. 73
 to publish statement annually.......... 39
 to turn over office, etc., to his successor 39
 same, in case of his death............. 39
 township fund loaned by................. 34

Trees, cut, etc., on school lands............ 75

Trespassers on school lands,................ 75
 liable to fine and commitment.......... 71

Truant officer............................ 96
 to report offenders...................... 96

Trustees of school lands............ ...... 31

Trustees of schools........................ 14
 accounts, etc., of treasurers examined
  by..................................21,37
 apportionment of funds by.............. 19
 body politic and corporate, a... ....... 15
 boundaries of districts changed by—
  at April meetings..................... 25
  bonded debt, how disposed of....... 28
  funds divided......................... 29
  liability for failure to divide funds.... 30
  property appraised.................... 30
  debts deducted from the same........ 30
  remainder of same divided............ 30
 same, appeal from action of trustees... 27
  how taken............................ 26
  who may appeal....................... 26
 same, election ordered in new district
  by.................................... 28

PAGE.

Trustees of schools—
  same, new map and list of tax payers filed by, within ten days, with county clerk............................................ 27
  clerk appointed by, who is also treasurer .......................................... 19
  same *pro tempore*............................ . 19
  debt, due school fund compromised by.. 22
  election of, conducted how..... ........ 17
  same, contested how.................. 17
  same, held for first time.............. 16
  same, notices of...................... 16
  same, ordered by township treasurer. 16
  same, polls opened and closed when.. 17
  same, postponed......... ............ 17
  same, tie, how determined........... 17
  same, time of....... ................15,16
  same, voters at, qualifications of..... 17
  election of, at town meetings........... 16
  eligible to office of trustee, who are..... 16
  gifts, grants, etc. received by........... 21
  judges of election...................... 16
  liable in a civil action—
    for failure to act upon notice of county superintendent.............11, 84
    for failure to distribute property in case of a division of a district...... 30
    for failure to return poll-book........ 18
    for failure to return statistics, or for false return of same...............12,84
    for loss of school funds................ 85
    for insufficiency of treasurer's securities ........................................ 84
  liable in a criminal action—
    for being interested in sale of school books, etc...................... .........2,85
    for conversion of school funds........ 84
    for perversion of funds to a sectarian use......................................... 85
  list of, furnished county superintendents by county clerk ............... 18
  map of townships, made by ........... 28
  meetings of, regular and special......... 19
  organization of board of............... 19
  president appointed...................... 19
  same *pro tempore*....................... 19
  quorum of............................... 19
  real estate, leased by...................22, 74
  purchased by............................ 22
  sold by................................. 22
  report to county superintendent.......19,20
  same, items............................ 20
  school house and site sold by........... 21
  same, title to, held by.................. 21

Trustees of schools—
  separate enumeration made by, when..20, 21
  successors to "Trustees of school lands"................................. 31
  term of office........ ................ 16
  title to school house and site held by... 21
  townships laid off into districts by..... 25
  treasurer appointed by................. 19
  same, removed by...................... 22
  same, sued by.......................... 22
  treasurer's accounts, etc., examined by. 21
  vacancy in office, how filled............ 17

Union school district dissolved, how........ 31
  funds of, put in hands of one treasurer...........................43,64,73
Use of school houses for meetings........... 45
U. S. flags on school houses ........102,103,104

Vacancies in office of board of education...49,52
  of county superintendent............... 8
  of directors............................ 41
  of trustees............................ 17
Validity of teachers' certificates ............ 56
Valuation of common school lands........... 76
Visitation of schools...................9,48,50
Vote of the people required to borrow money............................... 65
  to establish or discontinue a township high school...........................23, 24
  to levy a tax to extend a district school beyond nine months................... 46
Vote, etc.
  to locate a school house............... 46
  exception to the same................. 46
  to refund bonds or outstanding indebtedness .....................................66,67
  to purchase or build a school house...61,46
Voters of districts may add higher branches 57
  qualifications of...................... 17

Warrants, Auditor to issue to county superintendent............................9, 71
  paid by county collector............... 71
  return by same............... ......... 72
  refusing to pay penalty for............. 72
  See also "Orders."
Women may be school officers............. 86
  qualifications........................40,86
  to give bond and qualify as required by law .................................... 86
  may vote............................... 96

www.ingramcontent.com/pod-product-compliance
Lightning Source LLC
Chambersburg PA
CBHW030606270326
41927CB00007B/1071